Language Testing
RECONSIDERED

Language Testing
RECONSIDERED

Edited by

Janna Fox

Mari Wesche

Doreen Bayliss

Liying Cheng

Carolyn E. Turner

Christine Doe

ACTEXPRESS

University of
Ottawa Press

Library and Archives Canada Cataloguing in Publication

Language testing reconsidered / edited by Janna Fox ... [et al.].

(Actexpress, ISSN 1480-4743)
Includes bibliographical references and index.
ISBN 978-0-7766-0657-6

1. Language and languages–Ability testing.   2. Language and languages–Examinations.   I. Fox, Janna D., 1946– II. Series.

P53.4.L353 2007   418.0076   C2007-902093-3

Books in the ACTEXPRESS series are published without the editorial intervention of the University of Ottawa Press. The papers selected for publication in *Language Testing Reconsidered* were subject to a two-stage blind review process by experts in the field of language testing.

Published by the University of Ottawa Press, 2007
542 King Edward Avenue
Ottawa, Ontario K2P 0Z3
www.uopress.uottawa.ca

The University of Ottawa Press acknowledges with gratitude the support extended to its publishing programme by the Government of Canada through its Book Publishing Industry Development Program, by the Canada Council for the Arts, and by the University of Ottawa.

The editors gratefully acknowledge the support provided for publication of *Language Testing Reconsidered* by the Social Sciences and Humanities Research Council of Canada (SSHRC), the University of Ottawa's Second Language Institute, and Carleton University's School of Linguistics and Applied Language Studies.

Contents

LIST OF TABLES AND FIGURES

TABLES

FIGURES

ABBREVIATIONS AND ACRONYMS

ACTFL	American Council on the Teaching of Foreign Languages
AILA	Association internationale de linguistique appliquée *or* International Association of Applied Linguistics
ALTE	Association of Language Testers in Europe
ANOVA	Analysis of Variance
AUA	Assessment Use Argument
ATESL	Administrators and Teachers of English as a Second Language
CA	Conversational Analysis
CAE	Certificate in Advanced English
CEF	Common European Framework
CEFR	Common European Framework of Reference
CLA	Communicative Language Ability
CPE	Certificate of Proficiency in English
DA	Discourse Analysis
DIALANG	Diagnostic + Language
EAL	English as an Additional Language
EFL	English as a Foreign Language
ELD	English Language Development
ELP	English Language Portfolio
ELTS	English Language Testing Service
EPTB	English Proficiency Test Battery
ESL	English as a Second Language
ESOL	English for Speakers of Other Languages
ETS	Educational Testing Service
FCE	First Certificate in English
FSI	Foreign Service Institute
GPA	Grade Point Average
IDP	International Development Program
IELTS	International English Language Testing System

ILR	Interagency Language Roundtable
ILTA	International Language Testing Association
IMAGE	Illinois Measure of Annual Growth in English
ISLPR	International Second Language Proficiency Ratings
KET	Key English Test
LTRC	Language Testing Research Colloquium
MANOVA	Multivariate Analysis of Variance
MELAB	Michigan English Language Assessment Battery
NAFSA	National Association of Foreign Student Advisors
NFLC	National Foreign Language Center
NGO	Non-Governmental Organization
OE	Oral Examiner
OET	Occupational English Test
OPI	Oral Proficiency Interview
PET	Preliminary English Test
SLA	Second Language Acquisition
SLTP	Second Language Test Performance
SSHRC	Social Sciences and Humanities Research Council (of Canada)
TESOL	Teachers of English to Speakers of Other Languages
TLU	Target Language Use
TOEFL	Test of English as a Foreign Language
TOEFL CBT	Test of English as a Foreign Language Computer-Based Test
TOEFL iBT	Test of English as a Foreign Language Internet-Based Test
TOEFL PBT	Test of English as a Foreign Language Paper-Based Test
TOEIC	Test of English for International Communication
TSE	Test of Spoken English
TTW	Test of Test-Wiseness
TWE	Test of Written English
UCLES	University of Cambridge Local Examinations Syndicate
USIA	United States Information Agency
VPA	Verbal Protocol Analysis

ABOUT THE EDITORS

Janna Fox is an Associate Professor and Director of the Language Assessment and Testing Research Unit within the School of Linguistics and Applied Language Studies at Carleton University. She teaches courses in assessment, curriculum, and research methods. Her research interests are language test development and validation, and the interplay between assessment, curricula, and language policy.

Mari (Marjorie) Wesche is a recently retired Professor and former Director of the Second Language Institute and still active in the Education Graduate Studies program of the University of Ottawa. Her main teaching areas have been second language acquisition, assessment, and content-based second language instruction, with research emphases in second language vocabulary acquisition and assessment, language aptitude, performance-based testing, and immersion instruction.

Doreen Bayliss is the former head of Testing and Research Support Services at the Second Language Institute, University of Ottawa. Throughout her career, she has focused on test development and validation. Since her retirement, she has continued to engage in testing projects around the world.

Liying Cheng is an Associate Professor and a Director of the Assessment and Evaluation Group (AEG) at the Faculty of Education, Queen's University. Her primary research interests are the impact of large-scale testing on instruction, and the relationship between assessment and instruction in EFL/ESL classrooms.

Carolyn E. Turner is an Associate Professor in the Department of Integrated Studies in Education at McGill University. Her main focus and commitment are language assessment and testing in educational settings and more recently in healthcare contexts concerning access for linguistic minorities. She pursues these through her research, teaching, and service.

Christine Doe is in a doctoral program studying language assessment in educational contexts in the Faculty of Education, Queen's University. Her specific research interests relate to the use of diagnostic assessment to support learning.

INTRODUCTION

Janna Fox
Carleton University

Language Testing Reconsidered[1] is a collection of selected papers by several respected colleagues in the field of language testing, who engaged in animated conversation, dialogue, and debate at the Language Testing Research Colloquium (LTRC) 2005, in Ottawa. Part of that conversation is captured here. As the title of this volume suggests, each of the contributors has reconsidered language testing with the benefit of hindsight—looking back at its history, reflecting on personal experiences that highlighted key challenges or issues of concern, taking stock of both the limits and potential of current practice, and looking ahead to future possibilities. Central themes are evident across the chapters in this volume:

- the ongoing challenge of construct definition in language testing and the need for interdisciplinary research, not only within the narrow (and often inward-looking) disciplines of language testing and second language acquisition but also across the broader fields of applied linguistics/language studies and education;

- the expanding repertoire of research methods in language test development and validation, and the recognition of the important role that qualitative approaches can play in increasing our understanding of what tests do and what they measure;

- the evolving and increasing influence of social theory in language testing, and in reconceptualizations of the issue of *context* in test interpretation; and,

- the implications of the use of tests as decision-making tools—their limitations and potential.

As a whole, the volume provides a comprehensive account of issues of continuing concern in language testing and assessment from the perspectives of researchers who have, over the years, contributed in significant ways to the overall direction of the field. It captures the history of language testing, highlights useful methodological approaches in test development and validation, and elaborates a research agenda for the future. As one of the reviewers of this volume noted, "This account could not have happened earlier. Our field was due for this."

1

The first section of the volume is reserved for a paper by Bernard Spolsky and bears a famous question as its title — a question that has long been associated with him — namely, "What does it mean to know a language?" Spolsky acknowledges in his chapter, "On Second Thoughts," that this remains his "fundamental research question." In fact, as evidenced in the discussions across the other chapters in this volume, this question continues to challenge most language testing researchers. Spolsky includes in his paper some of the remarks he made in accepting the International Language Testing Association's (ILTA's) Lifetime Achievement Award at LTRC 2005. This is a remarkable chapter, wherein Spolsky recounts some of the key events in the history of language testing from the perspective of and in relation to his own professional life as a language tester (albeit, an "accidental one," as he points out). History and historian are intertwined in this paper, whether it is Spolsky's articulate lament for our lack of "historical sense" in consideration of current language testing issues; his long-standing concern over the ethics and consequences of large-scale, high-stakes "industrialized" tests; his intriguing discussion of the development of the "noise test" (with colleague Bengt Sigurd) as part of his early quest for "the chimera" of "overall proficiency"; or his recollections of thought-provoking discussions with William Angoff during long, treacherous winter drives between New York and the Educational Testing Service (ETS) in Princeton. His unique insider's view of language testing provides experienced language testers with a rarely shared perspective on the field and is an important frame for the other chapters in the volume. For those who are new to language testing, Spolsky's paper provides an impressive introduction to key questions, developments, and unresolved challenges in the field.

The second section of the volume, "What are we measuring?," consists of three landmark papers by Charles Alderson, Lyle Bachman, and Alan Davies, respectively. Each chapter probes and problematizes what language tests purport to measure.

Alderson, playing the useful role of iconoclast, attacks our soft assumptions about diagnostic assessment in his paper, "The Challenge of (Diagnostic) Testing: Do We Know What We Are Measuring?" Alderson points out that although language testers frequently mention diagnostic assessment, there is little or no consensus on this "rarely defined" and "much neglected" concept. Alderson situates his discussion of diagnostic language assessment within his work on the Common European Framework of Reference for Languages (CEFR), recent experiences with European assessment projects (i.e., the DIALANG project and the Dutch CEFR Construct Project), current theories of language use and ability, and research regarding formative/classroom assessment. Throughout, he highlights what we *do* and *do not* know about language development — knowledge that is essential for useful and meaningful diagnostic assessment and/or feedback. In this paper, Alderson takes the initial steps in his call for an aggressive research agenda to be undertaken by researchers across the fields of language testing, second language acquisition, and general education. He contends that such a comprehensive approach is long overdue and essential: if we are to clarify what it is to "diagnose" language development, we must first increase our understanding of it. This paper is a call to arms — similar to his call for research on *washback* (which was both a ubiquitous and largely under-examined concept before Alderson and his colleagues examined it). As such, Alderson's paper will certainly garner the attention of the field.

Lyle Bachman provides a comprehensive and thoughtful overview of the testing of oral language in addressing the question "What is the construct?" His paper, "What Is the Construct? The Dialectic of Abilities and Contexts in Defining Constructs in Language Assessment," begins with a review of language testing past, and a discussion of the differing approaches to construct definition that have been dominant within the field over the past 45 years. This historical perspective allows him to examine how the field has evolved in its definitions of abilities, performance, context, and task, and the interactions between them. He highlights the *dialectic* between what has been called *trait/ability-focused* and *task/context-focused* perspectives and examines how these perspectives have influenced the definition of constructs in language testing. Although socially informed *interactional* approaches may suggest a new synthesis to some, Bachman problematizes this notion by identifying important unresolved issues that proponents of a social view have failed to address. In the end, he discusses the implications of language testing past and present for future language assessment research and practice. This paper provides a richly detailed review of language testing and an incisive and well-articulated refutation of current arguments for a social turn in construct definition. It will stimulate ongoing discussion within the field for years to come.

The third chapter in this section is also a provocative one, which promises to engage its readership in considerable debate. In "Testing Academic Language Proficiency: 40+ Years in Language Testing," Alan Davies considers the construct of academic language proficiency as it has been operationalized in tests that were developed over the past four to five decades within the United Kingdom (and later Australia). He examines three attempts to test the English for Academic Purposes (EAP) construct:

1. the British Council's English Proficiency Test Battery (EPTB), developed in the late 1950s;
2. the innovative and experimental English Language Testing Service (ELTS) of the 1980s; and
3. the powerful, high-stakes International Language Testing System (IELTS), of the present day.

In his historical analysis, he links test development to changes in the definition of what language is and highlights sampling as a key issue in representing language use for academic purposes. Davies argues that there is little evidence to support the notion of a tenable EAP construct that is relevant to all students entering English-medium universities regardless of their disciplinary backgrounds or interests. He cites research evidence arising from studies of the three British tests considered in the chapter. Each defines academic language proficiency differently, but each accounts for approximately the same amount of variance (10%) in predictive validity studies. Thus, he argues, a construct of academic language proficiency may not differ in any appreciable (or measurable) way from less situated constructs of language use, precisely because tests — whether they claim to measure global/general proficiency or specific/academic proficiency — are unable to evoke the unique, highly situated relationships, interactions, and engagements that are characteristic of students undertaking academic work. His analysis and this paper directly challenge work on specific purpose language testing and will provoke ongoing debate.

The third section of the volume includes three chapters that examine new "Points of Departure." Each of the contributors to this section, Andrew Cohen, Anne Lazaraton, Lynda Taylor, and Tim McNamara, provides a state-of-the-art review of key approaches and new considerations in research supporting language test development and validation.

Cohen's paper, "The Coming of Age of Research on Test-Taking Strategies," begins this section of the volume with a comprehensive overview of the increasing importance of test-taker strategy research. He systematically examines the movement in language testing research from an exclusive focus on items and scores to an increasing focus on test-taker responses to tests, with particular attention directed at test-taker strategy use. Cohen discusses in some detail the conceptual frameworks that have been used over the years to classify types of strategies used and/or reported by test takers. He examines the contributions of verbal report research in helping us to better understand what tests actually measure and lauds this research for its direct contributions to arguments for validity. His review incorporates many concrete examples of test-taker strategy research and will be enormously beneficial to those new to language testing. It will also be of great benefit to those who wish to rethink and/or re-examine research on test-taker strategy use over the past thirty years in relation to the increased role that test-taker input is playing in test development and validation research.

Given the current, extensive use of qualitative approaches in language test development and research, it may be difficult for some to appreciate how limited a role qualitative approaches once played in language testing research. It is clear, however, in the chapter by Anne Lazaraton and Lynda Taylor, "Qualitative Research Methods in Language Test Development," that the growing presence of qualitative research methods in language testing research advances our understanding of both assessment products and the processes that contribute to them. In their chapter, Lazaraton and Taylor review key studies in speaking and writing assessment, which have utilized methods selected from what they refer to as the *qualitative toolkit*. Through practical example, systematic explanation, and discussion, they provide researchers with a comprehensive overview of how qualitative research tools have been used in the past for both test development and validation. Most importantly, they provide researchers new to these methods with not only an essential background regarding the range of options available for qualitative research but also practical, hands-on explanations of their use.

Tim McNamara's paper, "Language Testing: A Question of Context," completes this section of the volume. True to the volume's title, McNamara reconsiders his experience as language tester and language testing researcher in a thoughtful examination of context — what many consider the most challenging issue in language testing today (see Bachman's chapter, in this volume, for additional discussion of the issue of context). Unlike Bachman, however, McNamara examines context from the perspective of contemporary social theory. He uses the development and validation of the Occupational English Test (OET) as an example in exploring the paper's central premise, namely, "that all tests are tests of identity," because, according to McNamara, "all language tests are about identification." He contrasts traditional conceptualizations, which have attempted to characterize *context* in language proficiency testing but have ultimately failed to resolve the issue with those informed by social theory. In this paper, McNamara applies *subjectivity theory*, as developed in the work of Michel Foucault, in a reconsideration of the key properties of the OET in *context*. McNamara challenges the field of language testing to further explore social theory as an increasingly important explanatory resource for future language testing research.

McNamara's application of social theory in examining the OET provides a richly elaborated backdrop for the final chapter (and section) in the volume, Elana Shohamy's "Tests as Power Tools: Looking Back, Looking Forward." In section four, "Antecedents and Prospects," Shohamy situates her discussion of the power of tests within a personal narrative, beginning with reflections on her experiences as a test taker and describing how those experiences led her into language testing as a graduate student, at a time when language testing was just beginning to emerge as a field. Shohamy's passion and conviction as a language test *reformer* is evident in her account of the movements in her own research agenda from a focus on test development (methods and bias), to a focus on washback (how tests influence teaching and learning), to her current focus on social and political consequences of tests and their power. Her driving motivation in understanding tests and testing has always been "to possibly create better tests," but her understanding of what might make a test better has evolved from micro-consideration of the individual test taker, teacher, tester, and so on, to macro-considerations of the role of tests in education and society.

Like Spolsky, at the beginning of *Language Testing Reconsidered*, Shohamy relates her personal history as a language tester and researcher to developments in the field of language testing. She defines key issues that need to be examined "for a deeper and more comprehensive understanding of language testing" and elaborates a research agenda in the form of specific research questions that will address those issues. As such, she pulls together the themes that are developed across the chapters in this volume: the challenges of construct definition; the expansion of research methods in exploring what tests do and what they measure; the usefulness of socio-cultural/socio-historical theory in providing important new perspectives; and the implications of using tests as decision-making tools. In *Language Testing Reconsidered*, as Pearl Buck once observed, we face our future with our past.[2]

Language Testing Reconsidered has greatly benefitted from the generous engagement of its authors; from the feedback of respected colleagues in the field of language testing, who participated in the blind review process; and from the editors, who carefully examined each manuscript and provided suggestions to improve the overall quality of the book. *Language Testing Reconsidered* could not have been published, however, without the backing of the Social Sciences and Humanities Research Council of Canada (SSHRC), the Second Language Institute of the University of Ottawa, and the School of Linguistics and Applied Language Studies of Carleton University. Proceeds from *Language Testing Reconsidered* will support the work of the International Language Testing Association (ILTA), the organization of professional language testers and language testing researchers, who are committed to improving the quality of tests and who gather each year to discuss their research at the Language Testing Research Colloquium.

Janna Fox
Ottawa, 2007

Note

[1] The editors wish to acknowledge *Language Aptitude Reconsidered* (*Language in Education: Theory and Practice, 74*) (1990), edited by Thomas S. Parry and Charles W. Stansfield (Englewood Cliffs, NJ: Prentice Hall), which, as its title suggests, like *Language Testing Reconsidered*, stimulates further thought and research regarding language assessment.

[2] Pearl S. Buck, winner of the 1938 Nobel Prize for literature, once commented: "One faces one's future with one's past."

SECTION I

WHAT DOES IT MEAN
TO KNOW A LANGUAGE?

THE INTERNATIONAL LANGUAGE TESTING
ASSOCIATION
(ILTA)

Proceeds from the sale of this collection will support the work of ILTA. The International Language Testing Association (ILTA) is an independent association that was founded in the 1990s by assessment professionals who shared a general concern for fair assessment practices. Today, this concern resonates strongly among its members. A fundamental goal of ILTA has been to develop a Code of Ethics to inform ethical testing. The Code of Ethics, which was adopted in 2000, is neither a statute nor a regulation, and it does not provide guidelines for practice. Rather, it is intended to offer a benchmark of ethical behaviour by all language testers. ILTA further seeks to promote the improvement of language testing internationally through workshops, conferences, publications, and professional services. For more on the goals of ILTA, see p. 153.

≈ ≈ ≈ ≈ ≈ ≈ ≈ ≈ ≈ ≈ ≈ ≈ ≈ ≈ ≈ ≈

UCLES / ILTA
LIFETIME ACHIEVEMENT AWARD

The International Language Testing Association, with sponsorship from the University of Cambridge ESOL Examinations periodically awards the UCLES/ILTA Lifetime Achievement Award. This award is presented to distinguished contributors to the field of language testing who have demonstrated "extensive and inspirational service to the language testing community, and an outstanding record of scholarship." Past recipients of the award are:

> *Professor Alan Davies*, University of Edinburgh
> *Professor Lyle Bachman*, University of California, Los Angeles
> *Professor Bernard Spolsky*, Bar Ilan University
> *Dr. John L. D. Clark*, Center for Applied Linguistics, Washington, D.C.
> *Dr. Charles W. Stansfield*, Second Language Testing, Inc.

The introductory chapter of *Language Testing Reconsidered*, "On Second Thoughts," is based on Professor Spolsky's remarks upon receiving the UCLES/ILTA Lifetime Achievement Award at LTRC Ottawa in 2005.

≈ ≈ ≈ ≈ ≈ ≈ ≈ ≈ ≈ ≈ ≈ ≈ ≈ ≈ ≈ ≈

1   ON SECOND THOUGHTS

Bernard Spolsky
Bar-Ilan University

Abstract

An elderly student of language testing recalls some of the events in his career, attempting to relate them to current issues, and touching on such topics as overall language proficiency, the cloze and the noise test, the social responsibility of language testers, the development of industrial language testing, the danger of scales, and the value of knowing the history of one's field.

When I was awarded the rank of professor emeritus a few years back, a colleague kindly pointed out the real translation of the term: "e-" means out, and "meritus" means deserves to be. And when I learned in 2005 that the International Language Testing Association had decided to award me its lifetime achievement award, I took it as a clear confirmation that productive work was over.[1] I therefore feel no challenge to present new research here (in point of fact, the research that I have been doing since I retired has dealt not with language testing but with language policy and management) but to present some second thoughts on work that I did some years ago.

A Testing Tyro

In point of fact, I got into language testing through the backdoor: as a teacher, I became more and more suspicious of the relationship between tests and their results.[2] As a teacher-administrator responsible for a program of English for foreign students at Indiana University, my alarm was first aroused by the way in which we were using various kinds of tests. In particular, I became worried about the social consequences of using a test of English as a criterion for admission of foreign students to universities.[3] In an early paper, delivered at a conference of Administrators and Teachers of English as a Second Language (ATESL), the English teaching section of the National Association of Foreign Student Advisors: Association of International Educators (NAFSA) that preceded the Teachers of English to Speakers of Other Languages (TESOL), I raised a socio-ethical question: were we not, by using English proficiency as a criterion for admission of foreign students to American universities, limiting study in the United States to the children of parents well enough established financially or politically to make sure that they could go to the small number of good schools in their country which taught English reasonably well? At the time, in the late 1960s, it was generally held by English teaching professionals that English was for the elite: I heard many United States Information Agency (USIA) and British Council experts decrying the growing tendency to meet the burgeoning demand for English throughout the world by trying to teach it to everyone.[4] This experience confirmed my first realization, as a high school teacher in a largely Maori area in New Zealand, that teaching takes place in a social context and with constant social implications. It was shortly after that that I heard Robert Cooper's pioneering introduction of sociolinguistic criteria into language testing.[5]

But before I could fit that into my own work on language testing, I was attracted into the increasingly popular pursuit of the will-o-the-wisp of overall proficiency. During the time that I was at Indiana University, I became friendly with Bengt Sigurd, a recent graduate from the University of Lund who held a visiting lectureship at Bloomington.[6] In a conversation that we had after an otherwise unmemorable lecture, we wondered whether it might not be possible to test the overall proficiency of a second language learner by adding noise to a taped text. Thus was born the noise test,[7] and subsequent explorations of the relevance of reduced redundancy as a language testing tool.

In an effort to answer what has remained my fundamental research question ("What does it mean to know a language?"), we made use of the concept of redundancy developed as part of the statistical theory of communication (Shannon and Weaver, 1963). Three techniques, I argued in a paper that appendicitis prevented me reading at the Second International Congress of Applied Linguistics at Cambridge, England, in 1969,[8] had been developed that took advantage of this principle. One was the cloze, which had been proposed by Taylor (1953) as a way of determining the readability of a text, considered but rejected as a language testing technique by Carroll (Carroll, Carton and Wilds, 1959) in an unpublished paper,[9] and beginning to be used for language testing by Holtzman (1967) and others but not yet fully explored as it was to be by Oller (1972) and his students. The second was an intriguing attempt at a standardized cloze test called clozentropy (Darnell, 1968, 1970).[10] The third was the noise test itself (Spolsky, Sigurd, Sato, Walker, and Aterburn, 1968).

Each of these techniques had interesting continuing development. Oller's work with the cloze is well known,[11] and some of the doubts raised with it led to the subsequent development of the C-test (Klein-Braley, 1997). Douglas (1978) among others like Lowry and Marr (1975) kept up the interest in clozentropy. Gaies, Gradman and Spolsky (1977) followed up with the noise test. My own comfort with it faded when evidence emerged that some test-takers had excess of anxiety with the task of dictation with noise added.[12]

Finding Historical Context

Thinking back to those days, I recollect with sincere thankfulness my interactions with colleagues and students. My first important research was initiated in conversations with a visiting colleague and carried out with the collaboration of students. The first major language testing conference that I attended was at the University of Michigan, organized by Jack Upshur; other meetings followed regularly and finally were transformed into LTRC. What I later learned is that these meetings could be traced further back (see Spolsky, 1995, pp. 158–159); the first major language testing meeting was the session organized by John Carroll at the 1953 Georgetown Round Table (Hill, 1953), about which I had read while learning the historical context of the field.

I only learned about that meeting when I started on my research for the book that appeared 10 years ago (Spolsky, 1995). This originally was intended to be a study of the development of the Test of English as a Foreign Language (TOEFL). As I started to read the papers written for the initial planning conference (Center for Applied Linguistics, 1961) and especially the paper considered by many to be the first major work in language testing (Carroll, 1961), it became clear to me that I really did not know the historical background.

Coming into language testing in the mid-1960s, I had a fairly elementary view of the history of the field. With the daring of ignorance, I even had the nerve to put forward that view in a keynote address at the Association internationale de linguistique appliquée (AILA[13]) Congress in Stuttgart (Spolsky, 1977). I proposed that language testing had gone through three stages: an undefined stage of traditional testing, a stage during which structuralist linguistics and psychometrics had agree on a method of assessing knowledge of individual linguistic items, and the current period during which integrative testing (the term came from Carroll's paper) and sociolinguistics were leading to a new approach. The oversimplification appears to have been appealing and is still widely cited. But when in the 1990s I went back to read those earlier papers, I quickly realized how seriously I was suffering by not having learnt the history of my field.

Take a simple example. Many of us believed that Carroll's 1966 paper condemned Lado for not treating integrative testing techniques; read more closely, one sees that in fact he praised Lado (1961) for having adequately covered the field of item testing, making it appropriate to him to describe the additional value of integrative testing. I tried to make up for my mistaken assumption in Spolsky (1996) and in organizing the LT+25 conference, which celebrated the 25th anniversary of the appearance of Carroll's and Lado's pioneering works (Carroll, 1986).

So I ventured into history. For the first several months of a sabbatical, supported in part by a Mellon Fellowship from the Institute of Advanced Studies of the National Foreign Language Center (NFLC) at Johns Hopkins University,[14] sitting in a building in Washington, DC, just a block from where the 1961 meeting I was studying had taken place, or working at the Library of Congress or at the Georgetown University Library,[15] I sat learning what I could about the development of language testing in the years before I came into the field. The review took up half the book and gave me, I believe, a much clearer understanding of the development of our field.

This volume, with its interest in the past, is surely a place to complain about our lack of historical sense. Since my own excursion into the field, I have continually talked about history, finding in the 2000-year-old Chinese examination tradition,[16] or in the mediaeval northern Italian testing technique,[17] or in the late 17th century Royal Navy examination for promotion to the rank of lieutenant,[18] or in the mammoth examination introduced for the Indian Civil Service in the middle of the 19th century,[19] inspiration and explanation for current approaches to language testing. There are some scholars now, I am happy to say, who appreciate the historical approach. When one of them told me that he was teaching a course on the history of language testing, I sent him a manuscript copy of the first part of my book: he thanked me but noted that he planned to start his course just where I left off.

Of course, in general, we tend to cite only the most recent work in our field. For example, a recent journal issue devoted entirely to the ethics of language testing manages to cite Spolsky (1997) but ignores completely Spolsky (1981, 1984) in which I first use the term. And of course no one mentioned Spolsky (1967) which raised ethical questions about language testing. In the same way, discussions of reliability no longer refer back to Edgeworth (1888, 1890), or of validity of essay-marking to Sir Phillip Hartog (Hartog and Rhodes, 1935, 1936), or of the problem of scaling to the elderly Thorndike's dream of an absolute scale for language proficiency (Monroe, 1939), nor do our criticalists cite the impassioned attacks on the "encroaching power" of examinations expressed by Henry Latham (1877).

I suspect that it is our lack of historical sense and knowledge that condemns us to continually rediscovering the wheel. The current enthusiasm for testing is not new: in 1882, the Gilbert and Sullivan opera included this verse:

> Peers shall teem in Christendom,
> And a Duke's and exulted station
> Be attainable by com-
> Petitive examination.[20]

But competitive examinations by their very nature were limited to a small part of the population: like the Indian Civil Service examination or the Cambridge Tripos on which it was modeled, they aimed to select the very top candidates among a chosen elite. Psychometric theory made clear, as Edgeworth noted, that it was easier to make decisions at the extremes: a candidate who scored in the top 5% was clearly better than others. But at the centre of the curve, where most candidates are usually bunched, the standard error makes it very difficult to set precise boundaries.[21] This of course is just what happened when examinations were moved from the task of selection of the very best to the task of monitoring of the masses. This happened, it will be recalled, in the latter part of the 19th century in England, when the enthusiasm expressed by Gilbert and Sullivan was applied to developing tests to evaluate the effectiveness of mass elementary education. The door was thus opened both for efforts to establish standardized testing on the one hand and the development of the testing industry on the other.

Relations with Industry

Looking back, I am not sure how much I appreciated these changes before I made my excursions into history. As with many others in the field, most of my testing research was involved in developing small local tests. I certainly never assumed that the noise test would have commercial application, or that the functional tests that I worked on with my students (Spolsky, Murphy, Holm and Ferrel, 1971) would have other than local application.[22] But I was able to observe and to start worrying about the effect of industrialized testing even before I wrote my study. This was in 1967, when I became a consultant to the Educational Testing Service and the College Entrance Examination Board (they jointly owned TOEFL at that time) as member and later chair of the Committee of Examiners for the Test of English as a Foreign Language. During those three years, in short two- or three-day visits to the luxurious campus outside Princeton, I had a chance to learn the strengths and weaknesses of a large, powerful testing organization. Leaving aside the comforts (we were accommodated in the Princeton Inn, far beyond the Holiday Inn an assistant professor could normally afford), there was the opportunity of concentrated discussion about testing, not just with fellow university-based language testers but also with members of the senior research staff at Educational Testing Service (ETS).

I recall vividly several such discussions with William Angoff.[23] In one memorable icy car journey from the College Board offices in New York to Princeton, we talked about the strange phenomenon of the high correlation between the various parts of all foreign language tests: the only exception he had noted was Latin. This encouraged my continued search for overall language proficiency.

The weaknesses of industrial testing became obvious in our discussions with the test editing and production staff: they were constrained by the strict demands of the machines that controlled and evaluated their work. One such demand, as I later learned, was that every new test must be perfectly calibrated with all previous tests, a perfectly reasonable seeming requirement for a public standardized test, but one that meant that TOEFL was locked into the very first abnormal population (the particular students who were in large English as a Foreign Language (EFL) programs in the United States in the summer of 1962) on which it had been standardized. It also became clear how difficult it was to make changes in an industrial test—somewhat like steering a modern supertanker—and how little appreciation there was in ETS for TOEFL other than as a method of paying for interesting research in other domains.[24]

Pursuing a Chimera — Overall Proficiency

The conversation with Angoff brings me back to trying to understand what we were trying to do in those days. In those early days, some people in the field of language testing had come to it from psychometrics, but the majority of us came from applied linguistics—we certainly made sure that our doctoral students learnt more psychometrics and statistics than we had. There was a continuing and sometimes upsetting friction between the two, as we impatiently dealt with our areas of ignorance. At Princeton, interestingly enough, the local people were impressed and irritated by our psychometric sophistication, limited though it might have been. Unlike other committees of examiners, we were interested not just in content but also in testing. But within our own field, we were in the midst of the ongoing struggle to define the nature of applied linguistics and its role in dealing with real-world language-related problems.

Looking back, I see my own tension between the search for overall language proficiency on the one hand (witness the noise test and other work on redundancy) and the development of sociolinguistically relevant functional tests on the other as representing the same kind of bipolar attraction that the language sciences were struggling with. The language sciences were starting to bifurcate, with most following (or resisting) Chomsky as he set out to build a theory of linguistics that would justify it as a brain science, and another large segment following Labov (1972) and Fishman (1972) and others who investigated the social patterns of language use.[25] It is not too far-fetched to suggest that those language testers who pursued overall language proficiency were influenced by the language theorists, and those who started to develop functional authentic tests were influenced by the sociolinguistic model proposed originally by Cooper (1968) at the seminal meeting on language testing organized by Jack Upshur at the University of Michigan.

Unanswered Questions

Thirty years later, I still cannot give a short answer to the question, "What does it mean to know a language?" I have learned some of the characteristics that distinguish a native speaker from a learner, such as the ability to handle a reduction in redundancy. But I have also learned from colleagues (Davies, 1991) of the uncertainty of the concept "native speaker" and from my experience with the over-powerful Interagency Language Roundtable (ILR) scale, the problems produced by setting an educated native speaker as the highest level to be aimed at by a language learner.

What was originally called the Foreign Service Institute (FSI) absolute language proficiency scale (Jones, 1979b; Wilds, 1975) was developed, with the advice of John Carroll, to provide a method of encouraging diplomats to learn the language of the country to which they were being posted. The scale was aimed to rank the various language functions expected of a diplomat, starting with straightforward daily life in a foreign city, passing through the skills to handle simple diplomatic and consular business, and culminating in the ability to impress foreigners as speaking and writing the language better than they did themselves. In actual practice, it grew up as an evolving consensus between examiners and administrators, controlled all the time by the high status of their examinees, who were commonly higher on the pay scale than their language teacher-examiners. As time went on, the scale was adapted by other government agencies, each of which made their own local adjustments in scoring and administration without attempting to design their own valued set of functions. The problem produced is most easily demonstrated by the use of the scale by the Federal Bureau of Investigation. One of their tasks involves listening to the conversations of suspected drug-runners: thus, the ability to understand the colloquial Haitian Creole they speak or the mixture of Mandarin and Cantonese used by the Hong Kong gangs surely deserves to be at the top of their scale rather than closeness to the speech of a pedantic university literature professor. When developing its own graded framework of functional skills, the Common European Framework (Council of Europe, 2001) uses the term "native speaker" only once, when it set the goal of speaking in such a way that you can be understood by a native speaker.

The Council of Europe framework is exceptional in the exhaustiveness with which it sets out to list all the conceivable functional goals of foreign language teaching and all the known individual items that make up language knowledge. It is also refreshingly modest in its insistence that it is merely a guide to be used to develop a curriculum or test for specific purpose and context. In practice of course, it is no more validated than any other scale is (Fulcher, 2004a) and is as easily translated into rigidity.

The underlying question, as true of tests as of scales, is how to value results and translate them into interpretations. A fair criticism of the first 19th century spelling test was that it just counted the number of words correct without deciding which words are more important or more difficult. The work with modern vocabulary testing by Nation (1990) attempts to overcome this by using frequency as a criterion. In the early work that he did with scales, Thorndike (1910) developed a writing scale that consisted of examples of handwriting that had been ranked by several thousand teachers. Similar approaches were proposed for essays and other scaling, and in his own early work on oral testing, the pioneering Cambridge language tester John Roach (1945) made use of recorded samples to develop and train judges. While Thorndike himself agreed that averaging the scores of two separate judges leads to greater reliability, he also insisted that each be allowed to make a judgment based on their own criteria: a judge should be consistent, but there was no reason to expect judges to agree on a single scale. Clearly, he would disapprove of the techniques used by industrial testing concerns to see that their hired judges agree as closely as would computerized marking machines.

And of course the debate continues, in its most recent and sophisticated form in Bachman (2005). And it is just as well that it does, for I suspect that if ever we were to all agree on the nature of language proficiency and on how to measure it, we would simply build massive and powerful testing engines that would rapidly pigeonhole all our students.

Our lack of historical sense makes me wonder sometimes whether or not we are making progress. Attending our meetings, reading our papers and books, and comparing them with the work of our predecessors, I sometimes suspect that we have added techniques rather than understanding. The papers in this volume however will correct this over-pessimistic view, for they show that research in the field of language testing has been producing both new questions and new answers to some of the old ones.

In this paper, more of a memoir than I intended, I have been drawn unwittingly into some of the current debates but carefully avoided others; [26] on another occasion, granted a little more space or time,[27] I hope to speculate on future trends.

Notes

[1] As in Hamlet's reference to funeral baked meats furnishing the marriage table, this paper served a double function, being a seminar contribution and an award acceptance speech.

[2] My first testing publication in 1965 was a review of two tests.

[3] My second testing publication was a paper (Spolsky, 1967) at a conference of foreign student advisers and English as a foreign language teachers.

4 I recall the British Council and the USIA experts in Bangkok in 1967 agreeing that the way to improve the level of Thai English was to stop trying to teach it in elementary school.

5 Cooper (1968) was a byproduct of the major sociolinguistic study of the New Jersey Barrio (Fishman, Cooper, and Ma, 1971) that was underway at the time of the Michigan meeting.

6 Bengt Sigurd is now emeritus too, after a distinguished career in phonetics and general linguistics at the universities of Stockholm and Lund.

7 Spolsky, Sigurd, Sato, Walker, and Aterburn (1968) was first reported on at the Michigan meeting.

8 The subsequent publication of the paper (Spolsky, 1971) led several people to believe that I had been there. Among other sources of confusion for language testing historians, Davies (1968) was not a symposium in the sense of meeting, but a gathering of papers intended to give a picture of the state of the field (Kunnan, 2005a, p. 39); and the people listed as Department of Agriculture in Carroll's 1953 sessions at the Georgetown Roundtable (Carroll, 1953) were the early CIA language testers.

9 He thought it more likely to be a specific ability.

10 Essentially, he used a computer to compare a foreign student's answers to those of a selected group of American students studying a specific field.

11 For example, J. W. Oller, Jr. (1975, 1972).

12 It is not unreasonable to consider anxiety a form of noise. See, for instance, Vogely (1998).

13 AILA, the Association internationale de lingguistique appliqueée, was founded at the International Colloqium of Applied Linguistics at the University of Nancy, France. The English translation is the International Association of Applied Linguistics (also known as AILA).

14 Directed at the time by Richard D. Lambert, NFLC has since moved to the University of Maryland. Over the years, it and its offspring, the Center for Advanced Study of Language, have provided comfortable accommodation and stimulating ideas for my regular visits to Washington.

15 Georgetown inherited a vital collection of papers from the Center for Applied Linguistics.

16 I felt proud when I was invited to give a lecture on language testing at the Institute for Applied Linguistics in Beijing, a visit that gave me the chance to see the hall used for the final examination in the Forbidden City. And I enjoyed learning more about the Chinese origin of testing in Liz Hamp-Lyons' plenary at LTRC 2005.

17 I learned about Treviso and its policy of paying the schoolmaster by results from Madaus and Kellaghan (1991). It was a similar "closing of the circle" when I was asked to advise on the Treviso test being developed by the University of Venice and reported on by Geraldine Ludbrook at this LTRC.

18 One of Samuel Pepys' contributions as a naval administrator (Tomalin, 2003).

19 The arguments for replacing patronage with testing presented by Macaulay (1853) and others are worth reading.

20 *Iolanthe*, W. S. Gilbert, 1882.

[21] It is good to see the reference to standard error of measurement in the proposed ILTA Code of Practice.

[22] Of course, with the burgeoning of demand, a number of our colleagues have managed to start their own testing enterprises, raising a new set of ethical problems.

[23] William H. Angoff (1919–1993) was a distinguished research scientist at ETS for more than 40 years.

[24] Spolsky (2003) contrasts this with a quite different approach that developed in the 1990s at UCLES, where the language testers in charge made sure that the profits went back into language testing research and test evaluation and improvement.

[25] Labov, of course, always argued that he was doing theoretical linguistics and that the social information was needed to handle the variation that the generative linguists ignored, and Fishman of course never claimed to be a linguist but a Yiddishist studying the sociology of language.

[26] Such as the fascinating discussion of hotel bedrooms in recent lists, or the agonizing worries of government use of tests to return asylum seekers to their inhospitable homes.

[27] For example, Saville and Kunnan (2006).

SECTION II

WHAT ARE WE
MEASURING?

THE CHALLENGE OF (DIAGNOSTIC) TESTING: DO WE KNOW WHAT WE ARE MEASURING?

J. Charles Alderson
Lancaster University, UK

Abstract

The language testing literature is confused about the nature of diagnostic tests. *Diagnosis* is a frequently used but under-problematized concept and a debate is needed that might lead to a research agenda. This chapter aims to begin that debate by sketching out a possible set of dimensions of such a research agenda.

How does foreign language proficiency develop? Test-based diagnosis of language development should be informed by reference to theories of language use and language ability, even though second language acquisition research has failed to deliver a usable theory of development of foreign language proficiency. Research into formative and teacher-based assessment should be explored, both in language education and in education generally, for useful insights. Above all, we need to clarify what we mean by diagnosis of foreign language proficiency and what we need to know in order to be able to develop useful diagnostic procedures.

Introduction

In this chapter, I will argue that diagnostic testing is a much neglected area within the general field of language testing, both in terms of its possible function and in terms of the content and constructs that should underly diagnostic tests. Frameworks of language use and ability such as the Common European Framework of Reference (Council of Europe, 2001), American Council on the Teaching of Foreign Languages (ACTFL) (1985), and the International Second Language Proficiency Ratings (ISLPR) (Wiley and Ingram, 1995, 1999) provide encyclopaedic taxonomies and scales of relevant dimensions of language use and language learning that are likely to be implicated in and affected by language development. However, there is a relative scarcity, despite the scales that are presented in such frameworks, of evidence rather than speculation about their known relevance. Similarly, standards of language achievement, common in outcomes-based assessment (Brindley, 1998, 2001), which supposedly define the levels of attainment expected of (typically school-based) language learners, are often vague, ill-defined, lack any empirical base, and bear little relation to theories of second language acquisition. In short, it is far from clear exactly what changes as learners develop and therefore what diagnosis of second language development (or lack of it) should be based on, or how diagnostic tests might be validated.

Although I contend that such problems are of global relevance, increasingly authors and researchers emphasize the situated nature of knowledge, and the contextual constraints on how and what we measure. Therefore, I first need to contextualize my thinking, which has developed from my own work in Western and Central Europe. Before going on to discuss language development, diagnosis, theories of language use, and language ability, as well as other aspects of research in language education that might inform how we go about diagnosing foreign language proficiency, I therefore need to say a little about developments in Europe.

Context: Europe and the CEFR

For the past 15 years or so there has been increasing interest in Europe in language education and the transparency of certified language competence, for a variety of reasons. One major manifestation of these concerns and one major contribution to developments has been the Common European Framework of Reference for Languages, sometimes known as the CEFR or the CEF for short. The idea of such a framework is not new, both in Europe, where work began in the 1970s on developing definitions of a level of language proficiency that indicated that learners could operate independently in a foreign language — the Threshold level — and elsewhere in the world, as seen in the ISLPR, ACTFL, the Foreign Service Institute (FSI) and Interagency Language Roundtable (ILR) scales, the Canadian Language Benchmarks, and more.

Elsewhere the use of such frameworks, or outcomes-based statements, benchmarks, or national standards, as they are variously known, is controversial. Brindley in particular (1998, 2001) has shown the problems and dangers in using outcomes-based assessment, in terms of its impact on instruction. However, the CEFR is not part of national governmental policy; rather, it has been developed by an NGO, the Council of Europe, to broaden understandings of what is involved in language education. In point of fact, the Council of Europe has no power to impose anything on any member state, and it is at pains to emphasize that the CEFR is a point of reference, not a means of coercing teachers, nor even a basis for measures of accountability.

Nevertheless, the CEFR has already had enormous impact, and anybody working in or thinking about developments in language testing in the European context has to confront or come to terms with the CEFR.

The aim of the CEFR was to bring together a wide range of thinking and research in language education under a common umbrella, in order to contribute to increased common understanding of what it means to learn, teach, and assess a foreign language, and to give curriculum developers, teacher trainers, textbook writers, language test developers, and classroom teachers a common framework within which to communicate, to cooperate, and to develop independently.

The most immediate and pervasive application of the CEFR has been in the area of assessment, specifically that of portfolio assessment, proficiency testing, and, latterly, diagnostic testing. Indeed the levels of examinations provided by members of ALTE — the Association of Language Testers in Europe, to which Cambridge ESOL, the Goethe Institut, the Instituto Cervantes, and so on belong — are now expressed in terms of the CEFR.

The CEFR provides an encyclopaedic taxonomy of relevant dimensions of language use and language learning that are likely to be implicated in and affected by language development, which attests to the enormous complexity of foreign language acquisition. The CEFR itself is divided essentially into two: the so-called Descriptive Scheme and a series of scales. The former emphasizes the complexity of what it means to learn and use a foreign language. The CEFR views the language learner as a social agent, operating in specific social contexts. The learner's competence is described within a model of communicative language competence which owes a great deal to the Bachman model (Bachman, 1990), but much is made in the CEFR of tasks, their description, their performance, and the social purposes for which learners engage in tasks.

In addition to the Descriptive Scheme the CEFR also contains a series of scales across the four skills that describe language ability in terms of the six main levels of the CEFR and in a variety of settings (reading for information and argument, listening as a member of a live audience, writing reports and essays, informal discussions with friends, transactions to obtain goods and services, and so on). Such calibrated scales can be seen as providing a snapshot of development, and thus could be used as the basis for test development at the level of interest.

DIALANG

One application of the CEFR with which I have been closely involved is DIALANG, a project which has developed computer-based diagnostic tests in 14 European languages, in reading, listening, writing, grammar, and vocabulary.[1] The test framework and specifications for all the languages were based upon the Common European Framework, as that offered the most recent and most European basis for test development. It was relatively uncontroversial at the time and thus was most likely to be acceptable to the various testing cultures represented in the Project. Unlike other tests and examinations, the DIALANG tests were directly based *ab initio* on the CEFR rather than being merely linked to it *post hoc*, and DIALANG test results are reported in terms of the CEFR scales.

The DIALANG suite of tests was intended to be diagnostic and freely available over the Internet. Anybody can take the tests at any time and thus they are intended to be low-stakes — indeed no-stakes. They are intended to be diagnostic in at least two senses. On the one hand, they report results on each test in terms of the CEFR — from A1 to C2[2] — without giving any *score*. Thus they give learners some idea of where they are within the framework of the CEFR. Secondly, they are intended to diagnose ability within each macro skill area, in terms of sub-skills, which are reported in profiles immediately after the learner has taken the test. Thirdly, learners can explore their responses to individual items, to see what they got right and wrong and to speculate on why that might be so. Since the tests also encourage learners to assess their own abilities in terms of the CEFR (using *I can* statements) feedback is also provided on the match or mismatch between self-assessment and test results, explanations are provided for why there might be a mismatch, and advice is given to learners on how they can improve from one CEFR level to the next.

One of the problems the Project encountered was that, while the CEFR provided material to help define a number of content categories for item writer checklists, the Project had to complement the CEFR itself with material from the more detailed publications of the Council of Europe (the Waystage, Threshold, and Vantage levels), as well as from many other sources when designing the detailed task and test specifications — see Huhta, Luoma, Oscarson, Savaraga, Takala, and Teasdale (2002). However, detailed analysis of the results of the piloting on the English DIALANG tests (Alderson, 2005) reveals that there are virtually no significant differences across CEFR levels in terms of the difficulty of the diagnostic sub-skills that DIALANG endeavoured to test. For example, Alderson (2005) concludes with respect to the reading tests:

> Learners who achieved scores indicating they were at higher CEF levels showed weaknesses in all three sub-skills. It appears not to be the case that as one's reading ability develops, this is associated with an increased ability to make inferences, for example, rather than to understand the main idea. (p. 137)

Similar conclusions were reached with respect to listening:

> Even low-level learners are able to answer some questions that test inferencing abilities, as well as items testing the ability to understand main ideas. (p. 152)

To summarize, a set of diagnostic tests has been developed, based on the CEFR, which has proved to be very popular across Europe, but whose ability to diagnose development in terms of the CEFR has so far proved problematic.

The Dutch CEFR Construct Project

A better understanding of development might be achieved by a systematic inspection of language proficiency tests that have been developed and calibrated on the CEFR scales, to see differences across levels according to the test specifications and the test tasks. A recent project (Alderson, Figueras, Nold, North, Takala, and Tardieu, 2004, 2006) attempted such an analysis, in two ways. First, by taking all the descriptors common to a CEFR level for a skill (Reading and Listening) and analyzing these descriptors into their component parts, the Project developed a grid that could be used both to characterize texts, tasks, and items from a range of tests and to identify common features at each level of the scale across tests. However, so far, admittedly with a limited number of test tasks (75 in all) the Project has failed to identify such common features. Yet it may be that a larger-scale project, using the Project Grid, might accumulate enough evidence to contribute to the identification of key features at each level on the scale, which could then be examined for their power to predict development in the skills in question, and hence to have diagnostic potential. One promising attempt has recently been made by Kaftandjieva and Takala (2006).

The second part of the same Project collected test specifications and guidelines for item writers from a range of examination bodies, all of which claim to test language proficiency at different levels of the CEFR. Once again it proved impossible to identify elements in specifications and guidelines that were common to a particular level, and which were clearly distinguished from other levels. We conclude (Alderson *et al.*, 2006):

> There appear to be no systematic differences in the test specifications examined, in terms of most of the dimensions included in the Grid, as CEFR level changes. The specifications examined barely distinguish among CEFR levels in terms of content. (pp. 17–18)

When analyzing the results of expert judgments about texts and tasks using the grid, as well as examining the results of the inspection of test specifications, the Project found very little information on how different dimensions may affect difficulty, or how the dimensions may vary across CEFR levels. It was concluded that item writers' understanding of test specifications seems to rely in most cases on exemplification (previous exams) and local expertise rather than on any explicit construct of language development.

Indeed, I suggest that professional item writers might well have something to contribute to our understanding of how language develops. If item writers have some intuitive sense of what makes an item suitable for a given level of test, i.e., what will work at various proficiency levels, then an exploratory study would be worthwhile to see if experienced item writers can indeed predict item performance and then to develop ways to capture information on how they do it, if they can indeed do it. Anecdotal evidence suggests that experienced item writers can even write test items at an appropriate level for a language they do not know, combining their professional expertise with a native-speaker informant of the language. How this works, and what light it might shed on (intuitive) theories of language development, could also contribute to a better understanding of diagnosis.

State of the Art?

In summary, a body of evidence is developing that shows that the dimensions contained in the CEFR itself do not describe language development. Given that the CEFR is based upon a view of language learners that sees them as *social agents*, given that the perspective taken on language ability in the CEFR is sociolinguistic in its emphasis on text types, discourse types, task features, and the like, and given that the CEFR is deliberately intended to be neutral as to target language (there are no scales that describe how specific aspects of individual target languages might develop) then perhaps it is not surprising that the usefulness of the CEFR for diagnosing language strengths and weaknesses is rather limited. In light of the DIALANG and Dutch Construct Project experiences, it is suggested that "the CEFR in its present form may not provide sufficient theoretical and practical guidance to enable test specifications to be drawn up for each level of the CEFR" (Alderson *et al.*, 2006, p. 5).

Indeed, this is perhaps not unexpected in light of what Alderson (1991) says about language scales. He makes a distinction, since widely quoted and accepted, between assessor-oriented, user-oriented, and constructor-oriented scales. On reflection, it seems clear that the CEFR scales are a mixture of user- and assessor-oriented scales, but they are not constructor-oriented. This would account for the lack of guidance in the CEFR for the development of test specifications or guidelines to item writers. The user-orientation of the scales is apparent in the Can-Do statements: they are intended to inform users as to what a learner judged to be at level X (from A1 to C2) on the CEFR, can do. They are intended to help users — as in DIALANG — to interpret their test result. The fact that some of the scales are assessor-oriented (for example, several of the speaking and writing scales) has led to considerable confusion as to the status and orientation of the scales in general.

Language Development

In order to diagnose language development, we need to have a clear idea of how foreign language ability develops. It appears that the scales in the CEFR do not provide a clear picture of such development, and the Descriptive Scheme does not directly address the issue.

I would argue that any study of language development relevant to Europe should attempt to distinguish learners according to their competences as defined within the CEFR framework.

How does foreign language development take place? What do we know about development? We know that it is a long, slow, and complex business; that individuals vary greatly in how, how fast, and how far they develop; that development also varies by first language and probably by aptitude — at least in terms of *how fast* one learns. We know that development can be characterized in terms of how much one has learned — how many words *known*, how many structures *mastered*, how many phonemes produced accurately; we know that development will also vary by context of use: in slow, careful monologues, pronunciation, for example, may be more accurate (for certain phonemes and allophones) than in contexts where quick, spontaneous reactions are required, or on topics one has less knowledge of, or with interlocutors who are of higher status. We also know that development takes place in terms of quality, not just quantity: not simply the number of domains one can use the language in, but also the accuracy, appropriacy, and fluency of one's language.

We know that most learners do not develop native-like competence: the vast majority stop somewhere along the way. This fossilization of interlanguage can happen at any stage of development, and it may happen in some aspects of language use but not in others: pronunciation, for example, may fossilize earlier than lexis, while structural competence may cease to develop long before pragmatic competence.

So we know quite a lot, in general terms, about development, it would seem. We have frameworks, not only in Europe, of course, that purport to describe stages of development, usually in terms of the things that learners can do at a specific level, or tests they can pass. But what distinguishes a learner at one level from another learner at another level and how can a learner go from one level to another? Here there is less certainty: we describe learners at each level and say that learners go from A to B. But how do they do this? What do they have to do to get from A to B? What more do they need to learn or to do to get there (quantity)? How much better do they have to perform to develop from one stage to another (quality)? These are old questions, and it is common to characterize development as an ice cream cone in order to explain how the further up the vertical dimension you go, the more you have to do on the horizontal dimension, which sort of explains how development vertically takes longer the higher up you go — and which may even *explain* fossilization.

But what exactly do I have to put into my test or assessment procedure to decide whether a learner is at level X or Level Y on this ice cream cone? And, given that a test is necessarily only a tiny sample, in a very limited space of time, of the range of things that I could include in my language test, how can I be sure that I have sampled adequately?

These are all questions relevant to diagnosis: "How *do* learners go from A2 to B1?" What do they have to learn to make this journey? How can we advise learners on what to do, what to learn or unlearn? And how can we diagnose not only their level, as DIALANG claims to do, but also, using the normal definition of diagnosis as identifying strengths and weaknesses, how can we diagnose relevant strengths and, above all, weaknesses?

Diagnosis

We have seen that the CEFR does not of itself provide much insight into how language proficiency develops. Nevertheless it is increasingly used to characterize tests, proficiency levels, and learners. In addition, tests such as DIALANG have been developed not only to identify a learner's level in terms of the CEFR but also to diagnose learners' strengths and weaknesses. Indeed, DIALANG is fairly unique, at least in the European context, in attempting diagnosis. Language testers have long written about diagnosis as one of the main six purposes of language tests (proficiency, achievement, progress, diagnosis, placement, aptitude), yet we have presented no ideas how to design or research diagnostic tests. The literature on diagnostic testing is sparse and vague: it is common to assert that diagnostic tests are intended to probe the strengths and weaknesses of learners, but there is virtually no description, much less discussion, of what the underlying constructs might be that should be operationalized in valid diagnostic tests. Indeed, there is considerable confusion in the literature as to the difference between placement tests and diagnostic tests, and it is frequently claimed that diagnostic tests can be used for placement purposes and vice versa. The whole area of diagnostic testing is a much neglected area in language testing.

If diagnostic tests are supposed to identify a learner's strengths and weaknesses in language knowledge and use, what strengths and weaknesses are relevant? How should we identify these? Are they the same for all language backgrounds, for all learner types, for all possible reasons why learners might be acquiring a foreign language? Is diagnosis of problems in reading or listening different from diagnosis of problems in speaking or writing? Is diagnosis of pragmatic competence possible? Above all, what do we know about language development that could be relevant to diagnosis of language level or progression?

These are all issues that are rarely discussed or researched (for one exception, see Alderson, 2005). Not surprisingly, perhaps, in the light of such confusion and absence of a practical or theoretical rationale, no evidence is ever provided as to the validity of diagnoses, and to my knowledge nobody has described or discussed how the validation of diagnostic tests might proceed. In short, few have problematized — or even thought much about — diagnostic testing.

What we appear to lack, in short, is any theory of what abilities or components of abilities are thought to contribute to language development, or whose absence or underdevelopment might *cause* weaknesses. This is in marked contrast with other areas of diagnosis, be that in medicine, psychiatry, motor mechanics, or first language reading development, where not only do such theories exist, but also where there are well-established procedures for diagnosis of weaknesses and problems. I have been particularly struck by the long-established tradition in first language reading of numerous diagnostic test and assessment procedures. What many of these diagnostic assessment procedures have in common is that they tap into particular components of reading ability, for example, visual word discrimination, directional attack on words, recognizing sound-symbol relations, and more. They are also often noteworthy for the fact that they are administered individually rather than in groups and that detailed notes on performance are retained and referred to in interpreting results.

Diagnosis is also frequently related to remediation, where the results are acted upon by teachers, where weaknesses are addressed and efforts are concentrated on removing them. Indeed, in most diagnostic procedures I have examined, the administrator and interpreter concentrate on identifying weaknesses, not on strengths. Strengths seem to be taken for granted. At best they are seen as part of the background to the diagnosis rather than as leading to successful diagnosis and treatment. Whereas in our field we seem to be more interested in identifying strengths — what learners Can Do — rather than weaknesses — what learners Can Not Do. I suggest that in diagnostic language testing we should turn our attention much more to establishing what learners cannot (yet) do.

Many diagnostic procedures in other fields have less to do with the *real world* and holistic performance and more with being focused on isolating aspects of performance in a clinical setting. I infer from this that diagnosis need not concern itself with authenticity and target situations, but rather needs to concentrate on identifying and isolating components of performance.

A corollary of this is that diagnostic measures need not be integrated or task-based but might be more usefully discrete in nature, since the detailed interpretation that seems to be necessary for diagnosis is much more difficult in integrated tests or performance measures.

The evidence from what research has been done into diagnosis-related language assessment and the development of language use is that the components of test design that are typically included in proficiency tests and in frameworks like the CEFR are not predictive, at least in isolation, of stages of development. The evidence from the Dutch CEFR Construct Project is that dimensions of test design like text source, discourse type, text topic, and even the supposed mental operations tapped in test items do not discriminate tests that target different levels on the CEFR. The evidence from tests like DIALANG is that learners at A2 are clearly able to make inferences and understand the global meaning of texts, as are learners at C1. The difference lies not so much in the presence or absence, use or non-use, of the sub-skill but in the texts to which they are applied, and in particular to the *difficulty* of the language in those texts and the density of information. Thus I conclude from this that fruitful diagnosis will not seek to establish whether learners can read editorials in newspapers or understand adverts or recipes but will look at what causes any difficulties learners may have with such text types. I suspect also that whilst density of information, discourse structure, or lack of relevant background knowledge may be part of the problem, we are also likely to find that lack of linguistic knowledge, or lack of the ability to deploy that linguistic knowledge, may well be better diagnostic indicators.

Given our current lack of knowledge about what and how to diagnose, it is conceivable that insights into difficulties and weaknesses might usefully be gained from the learners themselves, through self-assessment and through awareness-raising activities. Asking learners directly what they think they have difficulty with, why they think they have problems in general or in particular, may well yield useful insights. DIALANG is one example of a supposedly diagnostic tool that offers learners the opportunity to assess aspects of their own proficiency, to receive feedback on their test performance, and to reflect on why there might be a discrepancy between their self-assessment and their test results. The system currently provides a set of possible reasons for such discrepancies, but it could conceivably be used in a more open-ended way in face-to-face dialogue between teachers/researchers and learners, both in terms of their understanding of the test results, their self-assessments, and the feedback the system provides, as well as in terms of what aspects of this array of feedback they think likely to be useful in their own language development, or which they have found useful in the recent past. Such dialogues may well provide new insights into which aspects of language knowledge and use can be diagnosed, and what sorts of diagnoses are understandable, relevant, and useful.

This latter point suggests directions for research agendas that might not only enhance our understanding of diagnosis but also might suggest ways in which diagnosis and diagnostic tests can be (partially) validated. I suggest that central to diagnosis must be the provision of usable feedback either to the learners themselves or to the diagnoser — the teacher, the curriculum designer, the textbook writer, and others. Thus the nature of feedback and the extent to which it can directly or indirectly lead to improvements in performance or in eradicating the weaknesses identified, must be central to diagnostic test design. Yet in language assessment in general we are all too often content with the provision of part or whole scores and a rather general description of what the scores might mean — in global terms. Diagnostic testing surely requires much more detailed feedback and explanation, and this represents a major challenge, not only to language testers but to applied linguists more generally. If the feedback currently provided, for example, by DIALANG or other diagnostic instruments is seen as inadequate, what better feedback can be provided?

Theories of Language Use and Language Ability

Any attempt to identify learners' strengths and weaknesses must, if only implicitly, relate to theories of language learning and use, and thus any approach to diagnosis must take cognisance of current debates in this area. Previous emphases on the importance of linguistic knowledge in language learning and the development of proficiency have to a large extent been superseded by more sophisticated notions of what language ability might be. The influential Bachman model (1990) of communicative language ability (CLA) saw language competence as consisting of organizational and pragmatic competence, with the former dividing into grammatical and textual competences and the latter into illocutionary and sociolinguistic competences. All these and their sub-components are presumably candidates for diagnosis, although nobody has yet explored this in any meaningful or systematic way. In addition, Bachman envisages strategic competence contributing to language use, consisting of the components of assessment, planning, and execution, and it is conceivable that aspects of such competences could contribute to diagnosis, if they could be identified. However, more recently it has been suggested by both McNamara (1995) and Chalhoub-Deville (2003) that this CLA approach is limited by being cognitive-psycholinguistic in nature, whereas language use has to be seen in a social context. Chalhoub-Deville argues that what she calls the L2 construct is socially and culturally mediated, that performances in communicative events are co-constructed by participants in a dynamic fashion, and that language ability is not static, or part of the individual, but rather "inextricably meshed" with users and contexts (2003, p. 376). Quite what the implications are of such theories for the very possibility of diagnosis are far from clear, but research into diagnosis and the concept of strengths and weaknesses cannot avoid taking these views into account, if only eventually to reject them as irrelevant or incapable of operationalization.

A related discussion has to do with the relationship between the constructs we aim to tap in language assessment and the tasks, or the means by which we hope to tap them. I accept the idea that ability and task interact, but I am agnostic as to where the construct is to be found, *pace* Bachman (2002). Clearly, the difficulty of a task and the measure of ability of an individual is a result of the interaction between task characteristics and individual characteristics. The rub is in identifying and characterizing these![†]

[†][Ed. note: For a historical review of approaches to construct definition in language assessment, see Bachman, Chapter 3.]

Bachman's position is that we need to take account of both task and construct in identifying language ability (as indeed do most volumes in the Cambridge Language Assessment Series, edited by Alderson and Bachman), but it is not clear how this would contribute to the identification of features of either task or construct that could have diagnostic potential. It is even less clear how the social interactionalist perspective of Chalhoub-Deville or McNamara would permit the notion of diagnosis or what its elements might be. Nevertheless, given the ongoing nature of the debate, diagnosis research should take account of these issues.

As we have seen from the CEFR, which is essentially task-based, such approaches to assessment have little or nothing to say about development, other than via Can-Do statements. One may be able to *read a recipe, phone for a taxi, write a letter of condolence, understand a lecture about nuclear physics*, but such Can-Do statements, and associated tasks, do not seem to me on their own to help us understand why one cannot do such things, and thus have little to offer of diagnostic value. Or at least the relevance of such task-based approaches to diagnosis has yet to be demonstrated, and the research reported in Brindley and Slatyer (2002), and Elder, Iwashita, and McNamara (2002) suggests that the adherents of task-based approaches themselves have no explanation to offer for the lack of consistent relations between task feature variables and individual performances (i.e., task features could not predict difficulty of task).

The interesting thing about such negative findings is that they call into question the assumptions of second language acquisition (SLA) researchers like Skehan (1998) that task performance can be predicted by a combination of aspects of code complexity, cognitive complexity, and communicative stress. It would appear that such a (relatively simplistic) approach to performance and hence to diagnosis is not very productive and that what affects performance — and hence what is worth diagnosing — is far from being well understood.

What is abundantly clear from the task-based language assessment research is that complex interactions of variables are to be expected in determining or influencing how individual learners respond to test tasks. In helping us reach such a realization, both the SLA literature and the task-based learning, teaching, and assessment literature have made a valuable, albeit as yet somewhat negative, contribution: we are not yet in a position to say what our tasks are measuring, or how less than perfect performances can help us diagnose weaknesses.

In the European context, where the CEFR is such a powerful framework and where CEFR levels are in many ways important milestones of language development, we lack a suitable diagnostic framework. What we need is a diagnostic framework that can interface with the CEFR, or a future revised and updated version of it, that can help us to explore how learners develop from one CEFR level to the next and how we can best diagnose problems in such development.

Formative and Teacher-Based Assessment

Since teachers are usually the ones who work most closely with learners, it makes sense to look at how they go about assessing their learners' strengths and weaknesses, and to explore what we can learn from them about diagnosis. Indeed, talking to teachers about how they diagnosed first language readers' strengths and weaknesses, as well as what sort of remedial action they took in light of diagnoses was how Clay (1979) began to develop her Diagnostic Survey.

> The difficulties which were demonstrated by the 6-year-old children who were referred to the programme were diverse. No two children had the same problem. Procedures for dealing with these problems were evolved by observing teachers at work, challenging, discussing and consulting in an effort to link teacher and pupil behaviours with theory about the reading process. (p. 67)

Until recently, there has been very little research into teacher-based assessment or any form of formative assessment in foreign language learning. However, Cheng, Rogers, and Hu (2004) show that teachers do indeed claim to use assessment to diagnose their learners' strengths and weaknesses, and thus looking at teachers' assessment practices could be a profitable way forward.

McNamara (2001) says that as language assessment researchers we should broaden the scope of our study to encompass classroom assessment, in order to make our work more answerable to the needs of teachers and learners. I would argue that looking at how teachers diagnose the strengths and weaknesses of their learners would also contribute to a better understanding of what can or could be diagnosed. Rea-Dickins (2001) takes up that challenge and shows how teachers go about formative assessment with English as an additional language (EAL) learners. Although descriptions of the assessment process are interesting, we are given little information on *what* teachers focus on and describe, and so future research questions that could contribute to our understanding of diagnosis are: What evidence for learning do teachers identify? What strengths and weaknesses do they concentrate on and what evidence has diagnostic potential?

Leung and Mohan (2004) use discourse analysis to understand how teachers do assessment, showing how teachers encourage students to discuss their potential answers to tasks, to justify and debate reasons why they think their answers are appropriate, to arrive at a group answer, and to understand why they believe their answers to be correct: the process is at least as important as the product. Teachers do not simply say *right* or *wrong* but treat answers as provisional and get students to reflect on why they might be correct or incorrect, often through a process of scaffolding students to find the correct answer.

Perhaps most relevant is the study by Edelenbos and Kubanek-German (2004), who develop the notion of a teacher's diagnostic competence, in other words "the ability to interpret foreign language growth in individual children" (p. 260). It is interesting to note that the authors claim that the advent of the CEFR and the related English language portfolio (ELP) "require language teachers to become familiar with new methods of assessment and testing" (p. 260). Specifically, they claim, teachers need to become "more aware of the fact that learners may be at different levels within various sub-domains of language competence" (p. 260). The ELP, they claim, "calls for keen observation and for a comparison between the perceptions — teacher and student — of a student's achievement. It also challenges the teacher to take a student's interpretation of individual progress into account" (p. 260).

However, yet again, the findings relate more to the process of teachers assessing learners, and much less to the actual content of the assessment. Future research into exactly *what* teachers focus on will be important in expanding our understanding of what can be diagnosed, given claims that teachers are in the best position to know their students and to have insights into learning. Insights gained from those closest to the learning — the teacher and the student — as to what changes as learners progress from level to level can only enhance our understanding of what to diagnose and possibly even how and when to diagnose, as well as what to do about the results.

General Education

If we go beyond the formative assessment literature into education more generally, there is a vast literature on learning that could be of relevance to diagnosis. I have already mentioned the literature in first language reading, for example, from which foreign language assessment could learn. Within our own field there is of course also a large literature on the learning of foreign languages, although much less of direct relevance to diagnosis. Broadfoot (2005) reminds us that learning is as much emotional as cognitive. She stresses that "if a learner likes and/or respects a teacher, if they are in a supportive group of peers, if the culture of the classroom is conducive to learning and, above all, how they see their own strengths and weaknesses, are factors that are likely to play a key role in the engagement and motivation of the individual concerned" (p. 131).

Thus, according to Broadfoot, it would be mistaken to see diagnosis as narrowly concerned with the technical aspects of language; we must be aware at all times of the emotional, the human, and, indeed, the social dimensions to learning and learning success. Broadfoot suggests that we need to see that "the context in which the learning is taking place, the degree of collaboration between teacher and student and between students themselves, the degree of confidence possessed by students, the opportunity for effective communication around learning" (p. 132) all contribute to learning success. We need in language learning in particular to remember the variety of learning contexts: the adult learning a foreign language for pleasure or tourism, the university student needing to learn a language to graduate, the school child forced to study a foreign language for which they see no need: all these different contexts are "significantly different affective contexts in terms of motivation, confidence and anxiety levels" (p. 134), that need to be taken into account. Broadfoot suggests that we need to deconstruct the familiar vocabulary of assessment and testing — "ability, performance, standards, achievement" (p. 138) and to pay attention to an alternative lexicon of "context, collaboration, confidence, communication and coercion" (p. 128).

However far this takes us from the notion of diagnosis is a matter of personal philosophy and interest, but when thinking about diagnosis we need to be aware that other disciplines might have something of relevance for us to consider. As Broadfoot says, "We should recognise that all learners are first and foremost sentient human beings and hence that the quality and scope of their learning is likely to be at least as closely related to their feelings and beliefs as it is to their intellectual capacity" (pp. 138–139). Assessment for learning, or even assessment as learning (Earl, 2003) is increasingly recognized as a crucial consideration in the development and use of assessment procedures.

The Need for Research

From what we have seen so far, it is clear that there is a need for research into foreign language development and diagnosis, at the very least within the framework of the CEFR, but conceivably much more generally. Certainly work within the CEFR will have to look for useful research findings elsewhere and then seek to apply them in the European context. In the USA, for instance, the work on measuring growth in second language proficiency mentioned by Butler and Stevens (2001) is of potential interest. It also appears that both California, with its ELD (English Language Development) test, and Illinois, with its IMAGE (the Illinois Measure of Annual Growth in English) could provide insights into what changes as learners improve their English.

We should also be looking at existing studies that have contrasted more or less proficient students to see whether the variables identified could have diagnostic potential within the context of the CEFR (see, for example, Yamashita, 2003, for second language reading, and Wu, 1998, for second language listening). But what should future research into diagnosis concentrate on?

Clearly we should not underestimate the complexity of language learning, and indeed we cannot as long as we pay attention to accounts like those of the CEFR, which constantly remind us of this complexity. At the same time, we should not despair and say that things are so complex that we have no hope of ever being able to describe language development or to diagnose components of it. There is always a danger of looking for single causes of development, of expecting that one or two variables will provide insight into strengths and weaknesses. It is highly likely, as with the diagnosis of medical or first language reading problems, that complex interactions amongst multiple variables will be of most interest, rather than simple bivariate correlations. Which is not to deny that there may well be useful indices or indicators of development, such as vocabulary size or pronunciation accuracy. These will probably not, however, provide useful diagnoses on their own.

We can learn from the diagnostic literature elsewhere which stresses that we need to understand the mental processes involved in learning a subject or acquiring a skill, something that applied linguistics rather lacks to date, with its current emphasis on social aspects of language use. For progress to be made in diagnostic testing, we will need to have a much better understanding of the psycholinguistics of foreign language learning and use. We need more of the sort of research being undertaken in listening, where considerable attention is being paid to bottom-up processes of speech perception and understanding, of short-term memory use, to attention and retention, where comprehension breakdowns are often shown to be associated with failure to segment sounds into words, and to lexical ignorance or deficiency, rather than exclusively concentrating on context and its supposed (and elusive) facilitating or inhibiting effects.

Clearly there are also non-linguistic factors that can help explain foreign language development, specifically aspects like motivation, both at a macro level in terms of so-called integrative or instrumental levels but also at the micro level of task motivation, and day-to-day, even minute-to-minute, motivation and attention. However, it is far from clear that motivation will be sufficient to explain specific strengths and weaknesses in development.

The SLA literature has suggested a host of other variables of interest in accounting for individual differences in acquisition, both cognitive as well as affective variables, including language aptitude variables, such as phonemic coding ability, language analytic ability, and memory. There are many potential candidates for further research, but it will be important to show that such variables have diagnostic potential in relation to language development. The same applies to matters of recent interest in applied linguistics such as language use strategies, or the difference between declarative and procedural knowledge.

Analysis of learner errors is not currently a fashionable area of research because of the well-known difficulties both of establishing what meaning the learner was trying to convey, and also the difficulty of describing and explaining the errors, but I have no doubt that the combination of error analysis with the creation and exploitation of suitably constructed large electronic corpora of learner language at defined stages of development will prove to be an immensely valuable tool in the near future. Such tools will need to be both longitudinal as well as cross-sectional in nature — already interesting research in this area is being conducted at Lancaster by Franceschina (2006) and Banerjee and Franceschina (2006), who are looking at the development of writing ability.

Alderson (2005) explores possible aspects of language knowledge — in particular grammatical and lexical knowledge and use — that might be worth exploring. It may be that the learner's current level of language proficiency influences the diagnostic potential of many linguistic, psycholinguistic, cognitive, or even affective variables. Thus, vocabulary size may have more diagnostic value at lower levels of proficiency, where a minimal vocabulary might be crucial to language use, whereas grammatical abilities may only become diagnostic once a learner has passed a threshold of lexical knowledge. Above all, it is fairly clear that the learner's first language will have a crucial role in mediating language development, and so diagnosis will have to take account of what is known about the language development and the linguistic strengths and weaknesses of learners from a range of different linguistic backgrounds.

There is no doubt that SLA has a contribution to make in this area, and indeed it has shown that it is fruitful to understand developmental sequences, for example the acquisition of negation, questions, tense and aspect, and more, as well as the development of pragmatic abilities. Clearly a learner's individual characteristics, developmental history, first language background, language aptitude, intelligence, proficiency in other foreign languages, motivation, and other characteristics need to be taken into account in such research.

I also believe that in Europe, it will be important to situate such work within the CEFR. Obviously the levels put forward in the framework are artefactual, and development is more a matter of progress along a number of different continua, and indeed backsliding along some of these at the same time as making progress along others. However, frameworks like the CEFR are useful in helping us to conceptualize and operationalize levels of proficiency, and since the CEFR has considerable currency in Europe in language education in general, it makes sense to attempt to relate descriptions of development and exploration of diagnostic utility, to the constructs of the CEFR. Ultimately it may well be the case that we need radically to revise the CEFR and our notions of what language development entails. But we can only do that by understanding the strengths as well as the weaknesses of existing tools, and seeking to expand their usefulness rather than dismissing them out of hand.

Alderson (2005) concludes by drawing attention to the advantages that computer-based assessment offers for the delivery of diagnostic tests, not least because of the possibility of the provision of individualized assessment, immediate feedback, advice, and even follow-up. One can imagine, for example, a learner inputting details of relevant personal characteristics like first language, age, learning history, and so on, and being presented with a diagnostic assessment tailored to such backgrounds. Bennett (1998) has suggested how computer-based assessment will eventually allow the embedding of assessment within learning, such that assessment procedures are indistinguishable from learning procedures. In such a situation we would indeed have developed tests with learning validity. However,

> before that day comes, we will need to have developed a much better understanding of foreign language development. If we can then incorporate such understandings into assessment and make them useful to learners through the provision of meaningful and useful feedback and follow-up, then diagnosis will truly have become the interface between learning and assessment. (Alderson, 2005, p. 268)

This seems like a huge undertaking, but given the claims for construct validity that underlie all language tests, it is surely indispensable. Given the need to relate diagnostic testing to learning, it is surely inadequate to consider that such coarse instruments as placement tests are capable of providing useful diagnostic information to learners. Much clearer thinking is needed in our field to define what we need to know in order to be able to provide adequate diagnoses for learners, on which useful feedback and advice can be given to assist with language development. Until we can do that I will be far from convinced that as a profession we have any idea what we are measuring.

Conclusion

In this chapter, I have argued that diagnostic language testing is a much neglected area. Although frequently named as one of the main purposes for language tests, there are very few examples of diagnostic tests, considerable confusion about the distinction between diagnostic and placement testing, and no theorizing about what might usefully be diagnosed. As a result we lack guidelines on how to construct diagnostic tests, what they might contain, or how to validate their use. In the absence of these, I speculated about what an adequate diagnostic test might look like and what it needs to achieve. A diagnostic test needs to be based upon a model of foreign language development, which we currently lack, which itself needs to be based on a theory of language ability and language use, about which there is still controversy. *Faute de mieux*, those constructing diagnostic tests in Europe have had recourse to a framework for language learning, teaching, and assessment that is widely referred to but which itself has limitations as the basis for diagnosis. We therefore need to complement our understanding of development by looking at other areas of assessment — in particular teacher-based formative assessment — for insight into what can be diagnosed, as well as to general education for current ideas on what facilitates and enhances learning. Taking account of these areas of education will doubtless enhance our understanding of what we might diagnose, but at the end of the day we need to account for the learning of *language*, and therefore we must work together with applied linguists, in particular second language acquisition researchers, in a joint search for variables that will help us describe, diagnose, and possibly explain foreign language development.

Notes

[1] The name DIALANG was a sort of blend of *diagnostic* and *language* testing; it is the name of a project, a suite of tests, and is the subject of a website: www.dialang.org.

[2] See Council of Europe (2001) for information regarding this six-point scale, ranging from A1 (lowest) to C2 (highest) as follows: A1, A2, B1, B2, C1, and C2.

3   WHAT IS THE CONSTRUCT? THE DIALECTIC OF ABILITIES AND CONTEXTS IN DEFINING CONSTRUCTS IN LANGUAGE ASSESSMENT

Lyle F. Bachman
University of California, Los Angeles

Abstract

Understanding the roles of abilities and contexts, and the interactions between these as they affect performance on language assessment tasks, has remained a persistent problem in language assessment. Approaches to this problem over the past half century have led to three general ways of defining the construct, or what we want to assess: 1) ability-focused, 2) task-focused, and 3) interaction-focused. While the different theoretical perspectives that underlie these approaches are not mutually exclusive, they are based on different sets of values and assumptions. Because of these differences, the conundrum of abilities and contexts and how they interact in language use and language assessments is, in my view, essentially a straw issue theoretically, and may not be resolvable at that level.

Nevertheless, the issues raised by these different approaches have important implications and present challenging questions for both empirical research in language assessment and for practical assessment design, development, and use. For research, they imply the need for a much more inclusive methodological approach, involving both so-called quantitative and qualitative perspectives. For practice, they imply that focus on any one of these approaches (ability, task, interaction), to the exclusion of the others, will lead to potential weaknesses in the assessment itself, or to limitations on the uses for which the assessment is appropriate. This means that we need to address all three in the design, development, and use of language assessments.

Introduction

A persistent problem in language assessment has been that of understanding the roles of abilities and contexts, and the interactions between these, as they affect performance on language assessment tasks.[1] The way we view these roles has clear implications for the way we define the constructs we intend to assess, and for the way we interpret and use assessment results. Furthermore, the way we view abilities and contexts — whether we see these as essentially indistinguishable or as distinct — will determine, to a large extent, the research questions we ask and how we go about investigating these empirically. In

41

the recent history of language testing,[2] one can trace a dialectic, if you will, between what has been called *construct-based* and *task-based* approaches to language testing (e.g., Skehan, 1998). Bachman (2004) has argued that these two approaches are quite distinct because they are based on different ways of defining the construct we intend to assess, and different assessment use arguments. They also use different approaches to the way assessments are designed and developed, and lead to different kinds of score-based interpretations. More recently, some researchers, drawing largely on research in social interaction and discourse analysis, have proposed an interactionalist perspective on language assessment, which views the construct we assess not as an attribute of either the individual language users or of the context, but as jointly co-constructed and residing in the interactions that constitute language use.

I will begin with a brief discussion of what I believe is a central and persistent problem in language assessment, that of relating abilities and contexts in the way we define the construct — or what it is that we want to assess. I will then provide a cursory historical — since the 1960s — overview of different approaches to defining what language assessments assess, which I believe illustrate a dialectic between what has been called "trait/ability-focused" and "task/context-focused" perspectives on or approaches to defining constructs in language testing. I will then discuss what I will refer to as an "interactional perspective" to defining what language assessments measure, pointing out some of the important issues that its proponents have raised, and what I see as some potential problems with this approach. I will then discuss some implications that an understanding of these differing perspectives has for language assessment research and practice.

Persistent Problem: Relating Abilities and Contexts

A number of researchers have discussed the problem of disentangling ability from context in language assessment. Bachman (1990), for example, described what he called the "fundamental dilemma" of language testing:

> Language is both the object and instrument of our measurement. That is, we must use language itself as a measurement instrument in order to observe its use to measure language ability ... This makes it extremely difficult to distinguish the language abilities we want to measure from the method factors used to elicit language. (pp. 287–288)

Similarly Skehan (1998), argues that the three underling problems of language testing are inferring abilities, predicting performance, and generalizing across contexts. For him, the dilemma, or what he calls the "abilities/performance/ context conflict" (p. 155), is that these problems cannot be solved simultaneously because each problem conceptualizes what is to be sampled differently. If the focus is on sampling abilities, for example, the performance and contexts are likely to be ignored or underplayed, and similarly if one chooses to sample performances or contexts.

Bachman's and Skehan's observations were based on and have stimulated a great deal of research in language testing that has investigated the relative effects of abilities/processes and test method factors/tasks/contexts. Bachman's perspective grew out of the trait-method studies that were conducted in the 1970s and 1980s, while Skehan's perspective has drawn more directly on the research in second language acquisition (SLA), particularly that on the effects of tasks on SLA.

Bachman (1990) and Skehan (1998) both point out that there have been two main approaches to solving this dilemma or conflict. One approach has been to "develop a model of underlying abilities" (p. 155), in Skehan's terms, which is essentially what Bachman called the "interactive ability approach" (p. 302). The other approach, in Skehan's terms, "is to bundle together the performance and contextual problems" (p. 155), which corresponds in essence to what Bachman called the "real-life approach" (p. 301). In the next section, I will attempt to demonstrate that language testers have indeed historically attempted to solve this dilemma or conflict by focusing almost exclusively on either ability/process or context/task in their approach to defining the construct to be assessed. Recently a number of researchers have proposed what I will call an "interactionalist perspective," which attempts, at least implicitly I believe, to solve all three problems simultaneously. In my view, one variation of this approach is essentially an extension or operationalization of the *interactional* part of Bachman's interactive ability approach, while the other variation is essentially an extension of performance assessment, in which the performance/context bundle is repackaged as *interaction*.

Defining Constructs: Historical Overview[3]

One way to characterize the recent history of language testing research and practice is in terms of the ways in which it has defined the construct to be measured.[4] From the early 1960s to the present, we can see a dialectic between a focus on *language ability* as the construct of interest and a focus on *task* or *context* as the construct.[5] This dialectic is illustrated in Figure 3.1, in which the focus of the construct is boxed. The dashed arrows trace the shift of the construct from ability/trait to task/content. I would hasten to point out that these different approaches were not strictly ordered chronologically. On the contrary, there has been considerable chronological overlap among the different approaches, both in terms of the theoretical statements of their proponents, and as they were played out in practical test development and use.

Figure 3.1: Approaches to defining the construct in language testing, 1960 to the present

		Focus	
Construct			
Approach / Major Proponents	*Ability / Trait*	*Task / Content*	
1. **Skills and elements** (Lado, 1961; Caroll, 1961, 1968; Davies, 1977)	Elements/aspects/levels Integrated language skills	Discrete-point, integrative tasks Taxonomy of language test tasks	
2. **Direct testing/ performance assessment** (Clark, 1972, 1978; Jones, 1985; Wesche, 1987)	Language proficiency: performance on tasks that approximate real-life language use tasks; Language performance in real life	Test tasks that mirror or duplicate real-life tasks Authentic performance	
3. **Pragmatic language testing** (Oller, 1979)	Pragmatic expectancy grammar	Pragmatic tests	
4. **Communicative language testing** (Canale & Swain, 1980; Canale, 1983; Morrow, 1979; Alderson & Hughes, 1981; Hughes & Porter, 1983; Rivera, 1983, 1984; Palmer et al., 1981)	Communicative competence General language proficiency	Meaningful communicative situation Authentic tasks	

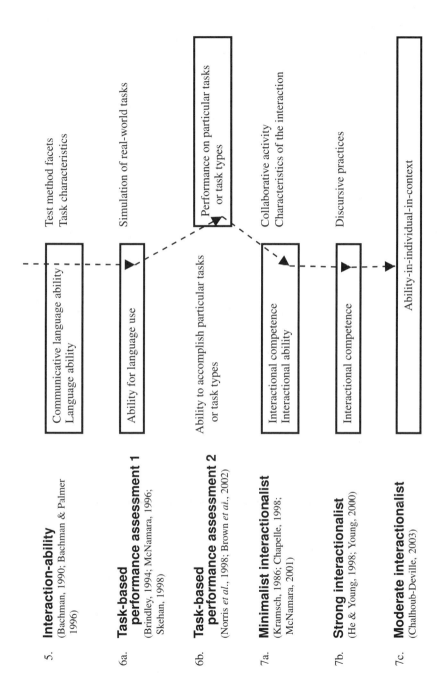

1. Skills and Elements

One of the first explicitly defined "models" for language testing was the "skills and elements" model that was articulated largely by Lado (1961) and Carroll (1961, 1968), and later by Davies (1977). In their formulations there was a clear distinction between skills and abilities, on the one hand, and approaches/ methods/test types on the other. Lado (1961) described the "variables" of language to be tested as comprising pronunciation, grammatical structure, vocabulary, and cultural meanings. He pointed out that although these elements can be tested separately, they never occur separately in language use. Rather, he stated, "they are integrated in the total skills of speaking, listening, reading and writing" (p. 25). Lado clearly distinguished the construct to be tested — integrated skills and separate language elements — from the situations or types of tests that are used. Indeed, he seems to have anticipated the current debate about task-based performance assessment in his statement that "a situation approach that does not specifically test language elements is not effective. It has only the outward appearance of validity" (p. 27).

Taking a position similar to Lado's, with respect to defining the construct to be tested, Carroll (1961) described this in terms of "aspects of language competence" (phonology/graphology, morphology, syntax, and lexicon) and skills (auditory comprehension, oral production, reading, writing). He pointed out, however, that "it would be foolish to attempt to obtain these sixteen different measures, for this would be carrying the process of analysis too far" (p. 34). With respect to the method of testing, Carroll stated that it is desirable to test specific points of language knowledge with what he called a discrete structure-point approach. However, he recommended that for testing rate and accuracy in the four skills, an integrative approach is needed. Such an approach requires "an integrated, facile performance on the part of the examinee," in which "less attention is paid to specific structure-points or lexicon than to the total communicative effect of the utterance" (p. 37).

In a later article, Carroll (1968) adopted the Chomskian competence-performance distinction (Chomsky, 1957, 1965), retaining essentially the same components of linguistic competence — aspects and skills — as in his 1961 article. However, in the 1968 article, Carroll argued that "linguistic performance variables" also need to be taken into consideration. In the second part of this article, Carroll elaborated a taxonomy of language test tasks, characterizing these in terms of dimensions such as *stimulus, response, modality, complexity,* and *task.* In the final part of the article, Carroll directly addressed the issue of the interaction between task, competence, and performance by introducing the notion of *critical performance,* which characterized, for him, the necessary relationship between the test task, performance, and underlying competence:

> If a language test is to measure particular kinds of underlying competence,
> its items must call upon language skills and knowledges in a critical way;

each task must operate in such a way that performance cannot occur unless there is a particular element of underlying competence that can be specified in advance. The extent to which this can be true is a function of the nature of the task and the specificity of its elements. (p. 67)

The skills and elements approach was perhaps the first approach in the history of language testing to explicitly draw upon both current linguistic theory and views of language learning and teaching. This approach to language testing was also the first to incorporate notions of reliability and validity from psychometrics. This approach thus provided a conceptual framework for defining the constructs to be tested that was based on linguistic theory and language teaching practice, and which was also in step with measurement theory at that time. This approach was extremely influential, and found its way into a whole generation of practical texts on language testing (e.g., Clark, 1972; Cohen, 1980; Davies, 1977; Finoccchiaro and Sako, 1983; Harris, 1969; Heaton, 1975, 1988; Madsen, 1983; Valette, 1967). Equally importantly, this approach also informed a generation of large-scale assessments of foreign or second language in the United States. Early versions of these include:

- the Advanced Placement Examination in French (Educational Testing Service),
- the Comprehensive English Language Tests for Speakers of English as a Second Language (McGraw-Hill),
- the Michigan Test of English Language Proficiency (English Language Institute, University of Michigan),
- the Modern Language Association Cooperative Foreign Language Tests (Educational Testing Service), and
- the Test of English as a Foreign Language (Educational Testing Service).

2. Direct Testing/Performance Assessment

Spurred by an intense interest, in both research and practice, in the testing of oral proficiency, the 1970s saw the emergence, largely in North America, of another view of the construct to be tested in the so-called *direct testing*. The term *performance assessment* was also used to characterize this approach (e.g., Jones, 1979a, 1985b; Wesche, 1987). This approach, according to Jones, who was one of its proponents, constituted a major sea-change from the approach advocated by Lado. Nearly twenty-five years after Lado's book, *Language Testing*, was published, Jones (1985a) wrote, "In Robert Lado's book ... we were admonished *not* to measure a person's speaking ability directly through a face-to-face test ... By comparison, direct testing today is becoming very commonplace" (p. 77; italics in original).

The published discussions of direct testing/performance assessment tended to focus primarily on the nature of the test tasks, which were claimed to mirror, or approximate real-life language use outside of the test itself (e.g., Clark, 1975). It was this replication of real-life language use tasks that was claimed to be the compelling evidence for the validity of such tests.

In defining the construct to be tested, proponents of direct testing/performance assessment referred to that as real-life language performance, which they viewed as the criterion for test tasks (e.g., Clark, 1972, 1979). Addressing the purpose of the Foreign Service Institute oral interview specifically, Clark (1972) states that this test "is intended to measure the adequacy with which the student can be expected to communicate in each of a number of language-use situations" (p. 121). For Clark, then, performance on a direct test was essentially a predictor of the language performance that could be expected of the test taker in real-life settings. Jones (1979a) took this definition of the construct a step further, explicitly identifying it with *performance*, and also emphasized the importance of prediction (Jones, 1985a). Scores from performance assessments were interpreted as predictions of future performance, and the evidence for validity lay primarily in the degree to which the test stimulus and the desired response, or both, replicated language use in real-life settings outside the test itself.

3. Pragmatic Language Testing

At about the same time as the *direct approach* was being promoted, but essentially independently of this, Oller was conducting a program of factor analytic research that led to his *unitary competence hypothesis* (e.g., Irvine, Atai, and Oller, 1974; Oller, 1976, 1979; Oller and Hinofotis, 1980). This hypothesis stated that language proficiency is essentially a single unitary ability, rather than separate skills and components, as had been proposed by Lado and Carroll. In the most extensive discussion of this research and the theory that underlay it, Oller (1979) identified the general factor from his empirical research as "pragmatic expectancy grammar," which he defined as "the psychologically real system that governs the use of a language in an individual who knows that language" (p. 6).

Having defined the ability to be tested, Oller then discussed the kinds of tasks that are necessary to test this ability. In a way that echoed Carroll's earlier notion of "critical performance," Oller described a "pragmatic test," which he distinguished from both discrete-point and integrative tests, as "any procedure or task that causes the learner to process sequences of elements in a language that conform to the normal contextual constraints of that language, and which requires the learner to relate sequences of linguistic elements via pragmatic mappings to extralinguistic context" (p. 38). Examples of pragmatic tests were the cloze (gap-fill), dictation, the oral interview, and composition writing.

Oller's conceptualization of the ability to be tested as a single, global ability, was, in my view, both simple and sophisticated. The notion of a single unitary ability meant that language testers did not need to concern themselves about testing the bits and pieces of language, while the notion of pragmatic expectancy drew upon current theory in both linguistics and pragmatics. Similarly, the types of tasks Oller proposed, such as the cloze and the dictation, were appealing to practitioners, since they promised to be both valid and easy to construct. The research upon which Oller's claims for a unitary competence were based was eventually rejected (see, for example, Bachman and Palmer, 1980, 1981; Carroll, 1983; Farhady, 1983; Upshur and Turner, 1999; Vollmer, 1980; Vollmer and Sang, 1983), and Oller himself (1983) admitted that the unitary competence hypothesis was wrong. Nevertheless, Oller's work has had a major and lasting impact on the field. In terms of language testing practice, his work was instrumental in reviving the use of the dictation and cloze as acceptable methods for testing language ability. His conceptualization of language ability as pragmatic expectancy grammar also foreshadowed later notions of strategic competence (e.g., Bachman, 1990; Bachman and Palmer, 1996; Canale and Swain, 1980).

4. Communicative Language Testing

At about the time the debates surrounding the oral proficiency interview and the unitary competence hypothesis were drawing to a close, or at least losing some of their heat, applied linguists in the U.S., Canada, and the U.K. began exploring a much broader view of language ability, drawing on a wide range of research in functional linguistics, sociolinguistics, discourse analysis, psycholinguistics, and language acquisition, as well as developments in communicative syllabus design and communicative language teaching.

Canale and Swain

Perhaps the first, and certainly one of the most influential papers to discuss the implications of this broadened view of language ability for language testing was the seminal article by Canale and Swain (1980). In this article, Canale and Swain adopted the term *communicative competence* to describe the ability that is of interest in both language teaching and testing. They defined communicative competence as "the relationship and interaction between grammatical competence, or knowledge of the rules of grammar, and sociolinguistic competence, or knowledge of the rules of language use" (p. 6). Canale and Swain explicitly distinguished communicative competence from *communicative performance*, which they defined as "the realization of these competencies and their interaction in the actual production and comprehension of utterances" (p. 6). In addition to grammatical and sociolinguistic competence, Canale and Swain posited a third component of communicative competence, which they called *strategic competence*, and defined as "verbal and non-verbal communication strategies that may be called into action to compensate for breakdowns in communication due to performance variables or insufficient competence" (p. 30).

With respect to the context, or kinds of tasks that should be used to elicit evidence of communicative competence, Canale and Swain indicated that "communicative testing must be devoted not only to what the learner knows about the second language and about how to use it (competence) but also to what extent the learner is able to actually demonstrate this knowledge in *a meaningful communicative situation* (performance)" (p. 34; italics added).

Canale (1983) subsequently expanded the Canale-Swain framework in two ways. First, he added *discourse competence*, which he defined as "mastery of how to combine and interpret meanings and forms to achieve unified text in different modes (e.g., casual conversation, argumentative essay, or recipe)" (p. 339). Second, he extended the function of strategic competence to include not only that of compensating for breakdowns in communication, but also "to enhance the rhetorical effect of utterances" (p. 339). Swain (1985) later refined the application of the framework to language testing by elaborating four "general principles of communicative language testing" (p. 36):

1. start from somewhere,
2. concentrate on content,
3. bias for the best, and
4. work for washback.

For Canale and Swain, then, the construct to be measured was clearly an ability or capacity that learners have. Their conceptualization of this capacity was much richer than those that preceded, and it initiated a major shift in the way language testers viewed the construct. They said very little about the specific contexts of tasks that should be used; rather, they suggested general principles for developing and using communicative language tests.

U.K. Symposia
At about this same time, a group of applied linguists with interests in language testing met in two symposia, one in Lancaster in 1980 (Alderson and Hughes, 1981, p. 7), and one in Reading, in 1981 (Hughes and Porter, 1983, p. vii). Both of these symposia addressed three broad themes:

1. the nature of language proficiency,
2. communicative language testing, and
3. the testing of English/language for specific purposes.

General language proficiency. At the first symposium there was very little consensus about whether there is such an ability as general language proficiency, with one participant denying that it existed, another wondering why it was even important to attempt to research it, let alone test it, and yet another declaring it a non-issue. If there was any consensus, it was that Oller's unitary competence hypothesis had generated both controversy and research, which was seen as positive, but that little was really known about language proficiency at the time, and that more research was needed. The discussion of general language proficiency in the first symposium was characterized largely by logical argumentation and not a little speculation, drawing on the experience and professional expertise of the participants. The papers at the second symposium, in contrast, focused largely on methodological issues about the way the empirical evidence supporting or rejecting Oller's general language proficiency factor had been collected, or presenting fresh evidence that purported to reject it.

Communicative tests. The discussion of communicative language testing at the first symposium consisted of responses to and discussion of Morrow's (1981) paper, "Communicative Language Testing: Revolution or Evolution." The responses and discussion in this section focused on two issues:

1. what constitutes a *communicative language test*, in terms of the features of the test itself, and
2. whether communicative language tests measure anything different from previous, traditional types of tests.

On the first point, Morrow's position was that communicative tests would necessarily involve performance that is "criterion-referenced against the operational performance of a set of authentic language tasks" (p. 17.). Morrow did recognize the problem of extrapolation, an issue that would also be a problem for performance-based and task-based approaches. Nevertheless, Morrow echoed the claim of the direct-testing proponents, stating that "a test of communication must take as its starting point the measurement of what a candidate *can actually achieve* through language" (p. 17; italics added).

The response papers and the discussion of Morrow's paper focused primarily on the issues of authenticity and extrapolation. In their responses, Weir (1981) and Alderson (1981a) essentially rejected Morrow's notion of *real-life* authenticity as a criterion for language testing. Weir argued that this is unrealistic for language tests, while Alderson argued that language testing constitutes a domain of language use in its own right.

Weir and Alderson, in their responses, also clearly articulated the problems of extrapolation and sampling. Weir stated the extrapolation problem as follows: "A performance test is a test which samples behaviors in a single setting with no intention of generalising beyond that setting" (1981, p. 30). Alderson points out the sampling problem as follows: "If one is interested in students' abilities to perform in cocktail parties, and one somehow measures that ability in one cocktail party, how does one know that in another cocktail party the student will perform similarly? The cocktail party chosen may not have been an adequate sample" (1981b, p. 57).

The theoretical discussion of communicative language tests at the second symposium consisted of a keynote paper by Harrison (1983) and a response by Alderson (1983). Harrison built his argument on an analogy between communicative tests and jam, beginning with the observation that, just as we should carefully consider the quality and contents of the jam we buy, so should we be wary of the tests we use. Drawing on the literature in communicative teaching, Harrison discussed several characteristics that should distinguish communicative tests, and a number of issues that he considered crucial in considering communicative testing.

In his response, Alderson (1983) begins by extending Harrison's jam analogy, suggesting that jam itself may not be a desirable product, and that one could well ask who needs jam, and by analogy, who needs communicative language tests. While he agrees with Harrison's warning not to accept as communicative any and every test that claims to be, Alderson goes on to systematically rebut most of Harrison's points.

The consensus view of these two symposia, in terms of the construct of interest in language testing, would seem to be more in terms of what it is not, rather than in terms of what it is. There was general agreement that the ability was not general language proficiency; what was to be tested was a set of areas of language knowledge and skills that interacted in complex ways in communication. What these areas of knowledge and skill were was not clear. On the issue of the context of language testing, there was general agreement that it was not *real life*, but something short of or different from that. Perhaps it could only be a representation of *real life* or perhaps language testing was its own context.

U.S. Symposia

At approximately the same time as the U.K. symposia were held, two symposia that also focused on testing communicative competence were held in the U.S. In 1979, what eventually became known as the first Language Testing Research Colloquium (LTRC) was held in Boston as part of the Annual TESOL Convention. The papers and discussions at this colloquium focused on methods, issues, and research in assessing oral proficiency/communication (Palmer, Groot, and Trosper, 1981). The empirical papers discussed results of studies into a variety of approaches to assessing oral proficiency. In my view, two things were particularly significant in this meeting. First, it brought language testers together with Michael Canale and Merrill Swain, who presented a short version of their 1980 paper, and thus set a research agenda for the next two years that would focus on efforts to empirically investigate the traits that were being measured by communicative language tests. Second, it introduced to the field of language testing, the research methodology of the multi-trait multi-method matrix (Campbell and Fiske, 1959), which would become, for the next few years, perhaps the dominant methodology in validation research in language testing. Bringing together a substantive theoretical framework of the construct to be tested, communicative competence, with a research methodology that was more sophisticated than the factor analysis of scores from miscellaneous language tests, provided the essential stimulus, in my view, for moving the field forward, beyond the unitary competence hypothesis and into the era of communicative language testing.

Another symposium on language proficiency and its assessment was held in Warrenton, Virginia, in 1981. Selected papers from this symposium that addressed challenging issues to language proficiency testing were published in Rivera (1984). The theoretical papers in the first part of this collection deal with the nature of communicative competence, how this relates to measurement models, and how integrative language proficiency tests could be improved by considering findings in communicative competence research. The papers in the application section of the volume include the results of empirical studies, or plans for such studies into a wide range of issues: the interdependency hypothesis of bilingualism that L1 and L2 proficiency are interdependent, the relationship between linguistic competence and communicative competence in a second language, the relationship of these to achievement in academic subjects, the effects of learners' background characteristics on the acquisition of linguistic and communicative competence, and issues in identifying an appropriate educational program for L2 learners with primary learning disabilities.

In summary, the formulations of communicative competence and communicative language testing/assessment that can be found in these discussions demonstrate a clear movement, in the field of language testing. This shift was from the apparent certainty of what was to be tested and how to do this that had been claimed by proponents of the skills and elements, direct testing/performance assessment and pragmatic approaches, to a new level of awareness of the complexity of both the ability to be measured and the contexts or tasks in which it might be measured. With this heightened awareness came a good deal of uncertainty. Communicative competence as an ability or capacity that individuals have, was seen as both a break with and an extension of prior notions of language proficiency, as defined in the direct testing approach, or pragmatic expectancy, as defined by Oller. Although the Canale and Swain framework was reasonably well defined, the richness and variety of the discussions summarized above illustrate the complexity of the notion of communicative competence, the lack of consensus on what it was, and the paucity, at that time, of solid empirical research into its nature. The contexts in which communicative competence could be assessed were vaguely conceptualized as *meaningful communicative situations* or *authentic tasks*. There was very little consensus as to what criteria could be used to identify such situations or tasks, especially if *real-life* tasks were the criteria for this. There was also a feeling by some that authenticity could not be achieved in a language test which, by its very nature, was artificial and inauthentic. It was definitely a new, if not so brave, world for language testers.

5. Interaction-Ability (Communicative Language Ability)

Bachman (1990, p. 113) conceived of performance on language tests as being a function of both an individual's language ability and of the characteristics of the test method. Nevertheless, he argued that in the design and development of language assessments, as well as in the interpretation of assessment results, it was essential to distinguish, analytically, the ability to be assessed from the assessment contexts or tasks in which language performance was observed. Further, he argued that it was essential to distinguish *observable* assessment performance from the *unobservable* abilities about which we want to make inferences.

In an attempt to address these issues in both the design and development of language tests, and in the interpretation and use of assessment results, Bachman proposed an approach that included two frameworks:

1. communicative language ability (CLA), and
2. test method facets.

Communicative language ability was essentially an extension of the Canale and Swain model, in which their notion of strategic competence was expanded from one that functioned essentially in accommodation and compensation to one that he hypothesized underlay all language use. He also reorganized their components of grammatical and sociolinguistic competence into *organizational competence* and *pragmatic competence* and elaborated these at lower levels of detail. Bachman (1990) saw *test method facets* as "analogous to the features that characterize the context of situation, or the speech event, as this has been described by linguists" (p. 111), and argued that these could "be seen as restricted or controlled versions of these contextual features that determine the nature of language performance that is expected for a given test or test task" (p. 112).

Bachman's two frameworks were subsequently incorporated into an approach to practical test development by Bachman and Palmer (1996), who renamed communicative language ability as simply *language ability* and the test method facets, *task characteristics*. Bachman and Palmer recognized, as did the proponents of performance assessment, that in order for score-based interpretations to generalize beyond the test itself, the characteristics of the assessment tasks needed to correspond to the characteristics of tasks in test takers' target language use (TLU) domains. Bachman and Palmer argued that by analyzing the characteristics of tasks in the TLU domain, test developers could use these sets of characteristics as templates for generating assessment tasks that would be representative of tasks in the TLU domain. The framework of task characteristics was thus seen as a way to solve the sampling problem of performance assessment, and to thus provide a stronger basis for making inferences to domains beyond the test itself. However, unlike performance assessment, the primary interpretation of test performance was about test takers' capacity for language use, rather than the prediction of future performance.

Bachman's and Bachman and Palmer's approach and frameworks provided richer descriptions of both the construct and the context than had previous approaches to language testing. However, even though both Bachman and Bachman and Palmer recognize and discuss language use in terms of interactions between ability, context, and the discourse that is co-constructed, their two frameworks are essentially descriptive, and provide little guidance for how they interact with each other in language use. Thus, while this approach may provide practical guidance for the design, development, and use of language tests, it does not solve the issue of how abilities and contexts interact, and the degree to which these may mutually affect each other.

6. Task-Based Performance Assessment

In the past decade, another approach to defining the construct to be assessed, *task-based performance assessment*, has been articulated.[6] As Bachman (2002) has suggested, there are two very different conceptualizations of this approach in the language testing literature. The proponents of one version of this approach (Figure 3.1: 6a. in left column) draw on the literature in communicative competence/language ability, communicative language testing, language for specific purpose assessment, and educational assessment, and explicitly build upon previous approaches, specifically communicative language testing and communicative language ability. Proponents of the other version of this approach (Figure 3.1: 6b. in left column) draw more heavily on the research that has focused on the role of tasks in second language acquisition, and the efficacy of using tasks in language teaching (e.g., Candlin, 1987; Crookes and Gass, 1993a, 1993b; Long, 1985; Long and Crookes, 1992), and link themselves explicitly with performance assessment, with little or no link with either communicative language testing or communicative language ability.

a. Task-based performance assessment 1

One approach to language assessment has focused on the kinds of tasks that are presented to test takers, the kinds of processes these tasks engage, and the abilities that are assessed (e.g., Brindley, 1994; McNamara, 1996; Skehan, 1998). The basis for these discussions is the premise that the inferences we want to make are about underlying ability for use, or ability for language use. Thus, Brindley (1994) identifies both language knowledge and ability for use as the construct of interest (p. 75). Similarly, McNamara (1996) discusses *construct* validity in performance assessments, while Skehan (1998) is explicit that the inferences to be made are about an underlying ability, or what he calls an "ability for use" (Norris, Brown, Hudson and Yoshioka, 1998, p. 1; Brown, Hudson, Norris and Bonk, 2002, p. 1). With respect to the construct that is to be assessed, this version of task-based language assessment differs very little, in my view, from that proposed by Bachman (1990) and Bachman and Palmer (1996). That is, in both approaches, the construct to be assessed is an ability or capacity that resides in the individual, even though the specific details of this construct vary from one researcher to another.

b. Task-based performance assessment 2

Another approach to language assessment has been articulated and studied most extensively by researchers at the University of Hawai'i at Manoa (Brown *et al.*, 2002; Norris *et al.*, 1998). The Hawai'i group, who describe their approach as task-based performance assessment, see this as a special case of performance assessment. This approach draws on research that has focused on the role of tasks in second language acquisition, and the efficacy of using tasks in language teaching (e.g., Candlin, 1987; Crookes and Gass, 1993a, 1993b; Long, 1985; Long and Crookes, 1992). In this approach, the construct to be assessed consists of "students' abilities to accomplish particular tasks or task types" (Brown *et al.*, 2002, p. 9). The context or tasks which they propose as a basis for their approach consist of "the simulation of real-world tasks, associated with situational and interactional characteristics, wherein communication plays a central role" (p. 10). Test takers' performances on these assessment tasks are evaluated "according to real-world criterion elements (e.g., task processes and outcomes) and criterion levels (e.g., authentic standards related to task success)" (p. 10).

The most salient difference between these two task-based performance approaches to language assessment lies not in the kinds of assessment tasks that are used, but rather in the kinds of inferences their proponents claim they can make on the basis of test takers' performance on assessment tasks. While the task-based performance assessment 1 approach aims at providing inferences about an ability or abilities that test takers have, the task-based performance assessment 2 approach aims primarily at making predictions about future performance on real-world tasks. The claims of task-based performance assessment 2 approach are essentially the same as those of the direct testing/performance assessment approach of the 1970s and '80s, discussed above. Specifically, the ability is performance on "real-life-like" tasks, and the assessment tasks are selected to "be as authentic as possible with the goal of measuring real-world activities" (Norris *et al.*, 1998, p. 9).

To summarize, the different approaches to defining the construct that have been discussed thus far can generally be seen as focusing on either an ability or abilities that test takers have, or on the types of tasks that test takers can perform. The approaches in Figure 3.1 that have boxed entries in the "Ability/Trait" column define the construct in terms of areas of language ability that test takers have, while those with boxes in the "Task/Content" column define it in terms of what test takers can do in contexts beyond the test itself. According to Upshur (1979), defining the construct as what test takers can do limits our interpretations to predictions about future performance. Defining the construct as what test takers have, on the other hand, can potentially tell us something about the nature of the ability itself.

7. Interactional Approach to Language Assessment

The last approach that I will discuss is the social interactional perspective, which has been articulated by several different researchers. Working largely within the area of the assessment of interactive speaking, and drawing on a variety of research literatures outside of language assessment, these researchers have identified a number of problems and lacunae in current conceptualizations of the construct, oral language ability, and how we go about assessing it. They present different, albeit overlapping, perspectives and suggest two general types of implications for language assessment: the need to rethink the way we define the attributes of participants in language assessments, and the way we define and operationalize the contexts in language assessment.

The way we define what we assess

Kramsch (1986), in a discussion and critique of the theoretical beliefs that underlie the notion of proficiency, as operationalized in the ACTFL Proficiency Guidelines,[7] is generally credited with the first use of the term *interactional competence*. Drawing on the research literature in psycho- and socio-linguistics, Kramsch stated that "the oversimplified view of human interaction taken by the proficiency movement can impair and even prevent the attainment of true interactional competence within a cross-cultural framework and jeopardize our chances of contributing to international understanding" (p. 367). Although Kramsch does not provide an explicit definition of interactional competence in this article, she defines it obliquely by stating what successful interaction presupposes "not only a shared common knowledge of the world, the reference to a common external context of communication, but also the construction of a shared internal context or 'sphere of inter-subjectivity' " (p. 367). She elaborates this further, arguing that "learning a foreign language ... entails not only language but also metalanguage skills in the foreign language, such as the ability to reflect on interactional processes, to manipulate and control contexts, to see oneself from an outsider's point of view" (p. 369).

Chapelle (1998), in an analysis of the relevance of construct definition and validation research to SLA research, draws on the research literature in validity theory in educational measurement to discuss three different approaches to construct definition — *trait*, *behaviorist*, and *interactionalist*. Chapelle begins by defining a construct as "a meaningful interpretation of observed behavior" (p. 33), arguing that we base this interpretation on performance consistency, and that "the problem of construct definition is to hypothesize the source of performance consistency" (p. 34). The interactionalist approach, which is of relevance here, explains performance consistency in terms of "traits, contextual features, and their interactions" (p. 34). Chapelle then goes on to discuss these three perspectives in detail, along with the implications they have for measurement, illustrating these with the example of the construct, *interlanguage vocabulary*. Chapelle argues that the interactionalist approach to construct definition must "specify relevant aspects of both trait and context" (p. 43). However, the interactionalist construct is not simply the sum of trait and context. Rather, "when trait and context dimensions are included in one definition, the quality of each changes. Trait components can no longer be defined in context-independent, absolute terms, and contextual features cannot be defined without reference to their impact on underlying characteristics [of language users or test takers]" (p. 43). For Chapelle, what is essential for making an interactionalist construct definition work is a component that controls the interaction between trait and context. This component, she further argues, is essentially what Bachman (1990) defined as *strategic competence* and Bachman and Palmer (1996) called *metacognitive strategies*. For Chapelle, then, an "interactionalist construct definition comprises more than trait plus context; it also includes the metacognitive strategies (i.e., strategic competence) responsible for putting person characteristics to use in context" (p. 44). She cites Bachman's (1990) definition of communicative language ability, which consists of "both knowledge, or competence, and the capacity for implementing, or executing that competence in appropriate, contextualized communicative language use" (p. 44), as an example of an interactionalist approach to construct definition.

Read and Chapelle (2001) describe a framework for vocabulary testing that draws on and extends their earlier work (Chapelle, 1994, 1998; Read, 2000). They present a framework for vocabulary testing that relates test purpose to validity considerations, from test design to validation. They then illustrate this framework with examples from the three different approaches to construct definition: trait, behaviorist, and interactionalist (Chapelle, 1998). Of particular relevance here is their application of Chapelle's (1998) definition of the interactionalist approach, with respect to vocabulary knowledge: "an interactionalist approach to *inferences* requires that vocabulary knowledge and use should be defined in relation to particular contexts" (p. 22; italics in original). They also discuss the implications for test use: "a new approach to *test uses* means going beyond tests designs to measure learners' knowledge of relatively decontextualized word lists and considering what other vocabulary assessment needs have to be met" (p. 22; italics in original).

He and Young (1998) and Young (2000) adopt Kramsch's (1986) term, *interactional competence*, and extend or refine it in terms of its components and how it operates in interactive speaking. He and Young (1998) begin with a discussion of assessing "how well someone speaks a second language" (p. 1), reaching the rather unsurprising conclusion that "defining the construct of speaking ability in a second language is in fact a theoretically challenging undertaking" (p. 2). Under the heading "Interactional Competence," they begin by describing speaking ability as "a subset of the learner's overall ability — or proficiency — in the language" (p. 3). Thus far, it seems that interactional competence is, indeed, an individual characteristic. However, they then state that "abilities, actions and activities do not belong to the individual but are *jointly* constructed by *all* participants" (p. 5; italics in original), which appears to mean that these abilities are not individual attributes. He and Young identify Kramsch's term, "interactional competence," with Jacoby and Ochs' (1995) notion of co-construction, which is essentially an interactive process by which cultural meanings are created. So now interactional competence appears to be a process. He and Young (1998, pp. 5–7) then describe the resources that participants bring to a given interactive practice:

1. knowledge of rhetorical scripts,
2. knowledge of certain lexis and syntactic patterns specific to the practice,
3. knowledge of how turns are managed,
4. knowledge of topical organization, and
5. knowledge of the means for signaling boundaries between practices and transitions within the practice itself.

He and Young state that "participants' knowledge and interactive skills are *local*: they apply to a given interactive practice and either do not apply or apply in different configuration to different practices" (p. 7). They then go on to argue that although participants' knowledge and interactional skills are local and practice-specific, they "make use of the resources they have acquired in previous instances of the *same* practice" (p. 7; italics in original). Thus, "individuals do not acquire a general, practice-independent communicative competence; rather they acquire practice-specific interactional competence by participating with more experienced others in specific interactional practices" (p. 7).

Young (2000) pushes the definition of interactional competence further in the direction of its being a characteristic of discursive practice, rather than of individual language users. "Interactional competence ... comprises a descriptive framework of the socio-cultural characteristics of discursive practices and the interactional processes by which discursive practices are co-constructed by participants" (p. 4). He contrasts interactional competence with the Canale-Swain (1980) framework. He characterizes the former as being based on a constructivist, practice-oriented view of interaction and competence, while the latter, Young argues, focuses on the individual language user (p. 5). He argues that the theory of interactional competence is characterized by four features:

1. a concern with language used in specific discursive practices,
2. a focus on co-construction of discursive practices by all participants,
3. a set of general interactional resources that participants draw on in specific ways to co-construct a discursive practice, and
4. a methodology for investigating a given discursive practice.

The resources that participants bring to a discursive practice are a recasting of the five (see previous page) that He and Young (1998) describe. Young (2000) again emphasizes the local nature of participants' knowledge and interactional skills, and that these are "distributed among *all* participants in a discursive practice" (p. 10).

My reading of He and Young (1998) and Young (2000) is that they seem to vacillate between conceptualizing interactional competence as an ability (i.e., resource) that individual participants bring to an interactional practice, on the one hand, and as an attribute of interactional practice that is locally co-constructed and shared by all participants, on the other. Similarly, the resources that participants bring to a discursive practice are both general resources that appear to be essentially aspects of or expansions of language ability (e.g., Bachman and Palmer) on the one hand, yet localized, in that participants tailor them to a particular interactional practice, on the other.

I would argue that this conceptualization of interactional competence as resources that participants bring to discursive practice is essentially the same as that of language ability as an attribute of individual participants. I would argue further that the notion that the competence is itself co-constructed and shared by participants, and context-bound, or local to a specific context, is highly problematic and not adequately supported by the research that He and Young (1998) and Young (2000) cite. Nevertheless, I believe that their perspective and the issues they raise provide an important contribution to how our conceptualization of language ability can be enriched, both in terms of what the various components are and in terms of how language ability interacts with specific contexts.

Chalhoub-Deville (2003) and Chalhoub-Deville and Deville (2005) provide probing and insightful discussions of the issues involved in an interaction-based construct definition. Chalhoub-Deville begins her forward-looking overview of the field by echoing Douglas's (2000) somewhat disheartening yet, in my view, accurate assessment of the current state of our field in terms of how we define the construct we want to assess: "while theoretical arguments and empirical evidence have ascertained the multidimensionality of the L2 construct, consensus is absent regarding the nature of these components and the manner in which they interact" (p. 370). She then spends several pages deconstructing Bachman's (1990) conceptualization of communicative language ability (CLA), correctly pointing out that this, by itself, is essentially a "psycholinguistic ability model" of "cognitive, within-user constructs" (pp. 370–371). Referring to the discussion in Chalhoub-Deville and Deville (2005), she contrasts the cognitive-psycholinguistic approach of CLA with a view of the L2 construct as "socially and culturally mediated" (p. 371). She proposes a construct, "ability-in-individual-in-context," which, she argues, represents "the claim that the ability components that a language user brings to the situation or context interact with situational facets to change those facets as well as to be changed by them" (p. 372). Chalhoub-Deville then discusses the *social interactional perspective*, arguing that this poses two challenges to language assessment: (1) "amending the construct of individual ability to accommodate the notion that language use is ... co-constructed among participants, and (2) the notion that language ability is local, and the conundrum of reconciling that with the need for assessments to yield scores that generalize across contextual boundaries" (p. 373).

Conceptualizing and operationalizing context
As with several of the approaches discussed above, proponents of an interactional approach define the context of assessment in different ways. Kramsch (1986) defines the context holistically as *collaborative activity*, while McNamara (2001, 1997) conceptualizes the assessment task or context in terms of *characteristics of the interaction*. Other researchers focus on the criteria for evaluating performance. Thus, Chalhoub-Deville (1995), Upshur and Turner (1999), and Fulcher (1996) discuss task-specific rating scales, while Jacoby and McNamara (1999) argue that we should consider the characteristics of indigenous assessments in developing criteria for rating performance.

McNamara (2001) discusses language assessment in its social context and articulates two of the interactionalist's main points. First, he argues that we need to reconceptualize the construct, language ability, recognizing that this is a social construction and that the way we define it embodies social values. Second, he argues for a richer conceptualization of context as dynamic rather than static. He correctly notes that "our existing models of performance are inadequately articulated, and the relationship between performance and competence in language testing remains obscure. In particular, the assumption of performance as a direct outcome of competence is problematic, as it ignores the complex social construction of test performance" (p. 337). Thus, while McNamara argues for a richer definition of the construct, he nevertheless clearly sees competence as an attribute of the individuals who interact with assessment tasks in performance assessment. Finally, McNamara challenges language testing researchers, particularly in the context of classroom assessment, to expand the notion of assessment, and he suggests two specific areas for further research and development:

1. "greater research emphasis on the implementation of assessment schemes, including an analysis of the impact of assessment reforms and a critique of their consequences," and

2. more adequate theorizing and conceptualizing of alternative, more facilitative functions of assessment in classrooms, which would involve "expanding our notion of assessment to include a range of activities that are informed by assessment concepts and that are targeted directly at the learning process." (p. 343)

Some Unresolved Issues Raised by an Interactionalist Approach

Just as the proponents of *interactional competence* or *ability-in-individual-in-context* have correctly pointed out the limitations of other approaches to defining the construct, most notably those of Bachman's (1990) and Bachman and Palmer's (1996) conceptualization of language ability, the interactional approach is not without its unresolved issues.

The relationship between interaction and language ability. It seems to me that the differences among proponents of an interactionalist approach to defining the construct can be characterized in terms of the claims they make about the relationship between interaction and language ability. He and Young (1998) and Young (2000), in my view, identify interaction, or discursive practice, with the capacity or ability to engage in such practice. Even though they discuss the resources that participants bring to an interaction, these resources nevertheless are characterized as local and co-constructed by all participants in the discourse. This, I believe, constitutes the strongest interactionalist claim: the interaction is the construct. Chalhoub-Deville (2003) argues that language ability interacts with and is changed by the context and the interaction. This view, in which the ability and context are distinct, with the ability changing as a result of the interaction, is a moderate interactionalist claim: the ability is affected by the interaction. A third claim is articulated by Chapelle (1998), who sees the capacity for language use (trait plus metacognitive strategies) as distinct from but interacting with the context to produce performance. In other words, for Chapelle, performance, or language use, is a product of both the ability and the context. While Chapelle notes that "the context dimension of an interactionalist definition must provide a theory of how the context of a particular situation … constrains the linguistic choices a language user can make during linguistic performance" (p. 45), she stops short of claiming that the ability is changed by the interaction. This, it would seem, is the minimalist interactionalist claim: the ability interacts with the context.

The strong interactionalist claim raises, it seems to me, some thorny issues. As Messick (1989) and Chapelle (1998) have pointed out, whatever our perspective (trait, behaviorist, interactionalist), what testers generalize from and attach scores and meaning to are consistencies in performance across a range of assessment tasks. Bachman (2006) makes essentially the same point about empirical research in applied linguistics in general. Thus, we might begin by asking about the source of the performance consistencies that enable researchers, whether in language assessment, discourse analysis, or SLA, to generalize. If the construct is strictly local and co-constructed by all of the participants in the discursive practice, this would imply that each interaction is unique. If so, what performance consistencies, if any, would we expect to observe from one interaction to the next? If we put the same participants in a different context, will their performances share any consistent features? Or, if we put different participants in the same context, what features, if any, will their performances share? If there are no consistencies in performance across contexts or participants, then we have no basis for generalizing about the characteristics of either. This problem has been pointed out by Chalhoub-Deville (2003), with specific reference to language assessment: "If internal attributes of ability are inextricably enmeshed with the specifics of a given situation, then any inferences about ability and performance in other contexts is questionable" (p. 376). She points to this as a challenge for language testers, to reconcile the local nature of language ability with the need for assessments that generalize across contexts (p. 373). If, on the other hand, there *are* performance consistencies, where do these come from? Since each discursive practice is uniquely co-constructed, performance consistencies cannot arise from the interaction itself. To what, then, are they attributable? Are these due to the attributes of the participants or the features of context? It would thus appear that this confounding of the roles of ability and context in interaction is problematic for generalizing, whether there are performance consistencies or not. If there are no consistencies in performance, any attempt to generalization is suspect. If there are consistencies, we are unable to explain or interpret them.

A second issue raised by the strong interactionalist claim is its identification of language use and language ability. The research literature upon which this claim is based comes largely from the various approaches to the analysis of oral discourse (e.g., sociolinguistics, conversation analysis, speech act theory, ethnography). In this research, the focus is clearly on language use rather than on the language abilities of the participants in the conversation or discursive practice. Young (2000) and He and Young (1998), for example, draw on the research in areas such as conversational analysis, linguistic anthropology, sociolinguistics, and speech act theory, all of which focus clearly on the speech event, the interaction, language *use*. In this regard, the same criticism could be applied here as Tarone (2000) applied to SLA researchers who take a narrowly "sociolinguistic or co-constructionist orientation":

> while ... [they] have a good deal of evidence showing that L2 learner's IL [Inter Language] USE is variably affected by identifiable features of the social context, they have usually not tried to show that those social features change the process of L2 ACQUISITION — specifically, the acquisition of an IL system — in any clear way. They have assumed it, and asserted it, but not often accumulated evidence to prove it. (p. 186)

The moderate interactionalist claim that language ability is changed by interaction raises, in my mind at least, questions about the generalizability and relevance of the research upon which the claim is based. Chalhoub-Deville (2003) draws largely on the literature in learning and cognition in building a case for the construct as *ability-in-language user-in context*. One perspective on learning that she discusses is that of situated/reflective learning, or what Sfard (1998) refers to as the *participation metaphor*, according to which learning is seen as a set of ongoing activities that are "never considered separately from the context within which they take place" (p. 6). Sfard contrasts this with the *acquisition metaphor*, which views learning as "gaining possession over some commodity" (p. 5), such as knowledge, concepts, or skills. If we want to generalize from the research in learning to language use or discursive practice, the first question that needs to be asked, I believe, is how strong a consensus there is in the field of learning about the nature of learning. If one can judge by debates in the literature (e.g., papers in Resnick, 1993) and recent overviews (e.g., Hofer and Pintrich, 1997; Saloman and Perkins, 1998; Sfard, 1998), it is clear that there is still considerable debate on this issue in the field of learning. Therefore, I would question the extent to which this research supports the moderate interactionalist claim. Although Chalhoub-Deville does not draw on the literature in SLA, she might well have cited research suggesting that acquisition varies as a function of context. Tarone (2000), for example, discusses a number of studies in SLA that suggest that differing social contexts affect what gets acquired and how it gets acquired. However, the research cited by Tarone was all conducted with L2 *learners*, so one must therefore ask whether the effect of interaction on the language *acquisition* of language learners differs from its effect on the language *use* of language users with native-like language ability. Thus, with both the literature in learning in general and with SLA, I would argue that we need to question the extent to which metaphors for *learning* generalize to *performance* or *use*.

Chalhoub-Deville also draws on the literature on situated cognition, which "focuses attention on the fact that most real-world thinking occurs in very particular (and often very complex) environments ... and exploits the possibility of interaction with and manipulation of external props" (Anderson, 2003, p. 91). But as with language use and language ability, one might well ask what the relationship is between cognition and knowledge, concepts, and so forth. That is, if cognition is an activity that is highly situated, what, if anything is the product of this activity. Furthermore, as with situated learning, within the various fields that constitute the cognitive sciences there appears to be considerable debate about the nature of cognition (e.g., Anderson, 2003; Roth, 1998). Thus, to draw on this literature to support the moderate interactionalist claim again would appear questionable.

And what about what I've called the *minimalist interactionalist* claim? As with proponents of the strong and moderate interactionalist claims, Chapelle (1998) also discusses a number of challenges that an interactionalist approach poses, not only for language testers but for SLA researchers as well. For example, she points out that content analysis, as an empirical validation method, "requires that the person and context sources of learner's performance in the operational setting be hypothesized, but the analytic procedures for making such process-oriented hypotheses have not yet been developed" (pp. 64–65). Similarly, empirical item analysis requires that the researcher operationalize both context and person variables, as well as their interaction, but such operational definitions have not been specified (p. 65). Finally, she refers to Messick's measurement *conundrum*: "strategies can vary across people and tasks even when the same results are achieved" (p. 65). I will return to this last point below as something that differentiates language testers as practitioners from language testers as researchers.

I have argued that the research that has been cited in support of the strong and moderate interactionalist claims is either controversial in the fields from which they are drawn or of questionable relevance to these claims. I have also argued, as have the proponents of all three types of interactionalist claims, that the research evidence in support of any of these claims, in the context of language assessment, is scanty, if not non-existent. What I have *not* argued is that these claims are wrong. I have pointed out what I believe are some unresolved issues with these claims, as have their proponents. Chapelle (1998), Young (2000), McNamara (2001), and Chalhoub-Deville (2003) all discuss challenges that an interactionalist approach poses for language assessment, and these challenges imply a research agenda for future language testers. On this point I am in complete agreement with them, and list in the following section, some unanswered questions that might help focus such research. These are not, of course, entirely new questions, and some research has been conducted on virtually each of them. What has not happened, I believe, is for these questions to be investigated carefully in the context of language assessment.

Some Implications for Language Assessment

Each of the different approaches to defining the construct of interest that have been discussed above have drawn on research literatures outside language testing. However, I believe that it is the interactionalist approach, which has drawn on research approaches and perspectives that are in the starkest contrast to those generally associated with language assessment, that poses the most serious and interesting challenges for the field. But in order to appropriately translate these challenges into implications for language testing, I believe that we must first distinguish two roles of language testers that Bachman (1990) pointed out: the language testing practitioner and the language testing researcher. The fact that the majority of language testing researchers are also practitioners does not lessen the importance of the difference between these two roles.

Language Testers as Researchers and as Practitioners

Perhaps the most important distinction between the roles of language testing researcher and practitioner is that of purpose, or goal. The language testing researcher's goal, I believe, is to better understand, *inter alia*, the psychological and contextual factors that affect performance on language assessments, the types of language use that language assessments elicit, the relationship between language use elicited in assessments and that created in *real-life* settings, and the relationship between the abilities engaged in language assessments and those engaged in *real-life* settings. I would argue that the goal of the language testing practitioner, on the other hand, is to design and develop language assessments that are useful for their intended purposes. In either role, I believe that it is essential that we clearly define what it is we want to measure or what we want to investigate.

Because of these differing purposes, practitioners and researchers may investigate different constructs, may define the constructs of interest with different degrees of specificity, and may investigate differing ranges of constructs. When we language testers wear our researcher hat, we are essentially applied linguists who are seeking to expand our knowledge. What we choose to investigate, or observe, as well as how we define this, how we choose to observe it, and how we interpret it, will be influenced by a number of different dimensions, including our perspective on knowledge, our purpose, where we place ourselves in defining constructs and contexts and the relationship between these, and our view of the world (Bachman, 2006). As researchers, we are interested in both the *how* and *why* questions. For example:

- How do the features of a graphic prompt influence the kinds of oral language test takers produce, and why?
- How do test takers interact with and respond differently to different types of tasks based on a reading passage, and why?
- How do ESL teachers in elementary schools interpret and use standards-based assessments, and why?
- How do test takers with different personality traits interact with each other in a group oral discussion assessment, and why do they interact this way?

More often than not, we can find tentative answers to the how questions, and are left to speculate on the why. Thus, as researchers, we have the luxury of investigating not only constructs defined in very precise ways but also a large range of these in a single study. We can also investigate constructs that we only hypothesize to be relevant to test performance. Finally, the impact of our research is generally minimal, typically being limited to other researchers, journal reviewers, reviewers of grant proposals, and tenure and promotion committees.

As language testing practitioners, on the other hand, we work under a very different set of constraints. First of all, we may be held accountable for the decisions that are made on the basis of our test, and the higher the stakes of the decisions, the greater the burden of accountability. Thus, if the decisions that are made on the basis of the test will have a major impact on the lives of test takers (high stakes), then the language testing practitioner must collect considerable evidence to support these decisions. Because of this burden of accountability, language testing practitioners must deal with *known* constructs that may be defined very broadly. Thus, while a researcher might be interested in the internal construction of meaning formed by interacting with a written text, the practitioner is more likely to be interested in reading comprehension. Part of the accountability equation involves practicality, so the language testing practitioner must generally focus on constructs that are directly relevant to the decisions that are to be made. Thus, while the researcher might be able to investigate the effects of different personality types on oral test performance, the practitioner may not have the resources, such as time, personnel, expertise, or funding, to include the assessment of personality type in his assessment. While the researcher may have resources to collect verbal protocols from test takers and to analyze the discourse they produce, the practitioner will seldom have the resources for this, or be able to justify using them in this way. In using the measurement models and statistical tools needed to provide accountability, the practitioner must generally work with interpretations that are group-based. Thus, even though research tells us that each test taker may approach the same reading passage and questions differently, interact with these differently, and draw on different areas of knowledge, processes, or strategies in responding to the questions, the practitioner must assume that the scores of test takers on this reading test can all be interpreted in the same way: level of reading ability. The language testing practitioner is thus interested in the *what* and *how much* questions. For example:

- What does this test score tell us about what test takers know or can do?
- How much of this do different test takers have, or how well can different test takers do it?
- What kind and how much impact will our intended decisions have on stakeholders?

When the language testing practitioner investigates these questions, he is attempting to answer questions about the reliability of the scores, the validity of the interpretations, and the fairness and appropriateness of the decisions that are made. He is preparing to be held accountable by stakeholders.

Implications for language testing researchers

The approaches to language testing that have been discussed above have been based not only on theoretical perspectives drawn from other disciplines but also on empirical research. If we were to examine this research closely, I believe we would see that both the types of research questions that have been investigated and the specific research approaches that have been used derive largely from differences in several dimensions of research. These dimensions are discussed by Bachman (2006), and although these are framed broadly within empirical research in applied linguistics, I believe that they also apply to research in language testing. The lesson to be learned here, I believe, is that the issues and questions in language testing research are far too complex, and the perspectives that are involved far too diverse to admit to any doctrinaire positions, with respect to either what the *true* construct is or what the *correct* methodological approach is.

Consideration of the historical dialectic in language assessment between abilities and contexts, and of the interactionalist perspective in particular, also raises a host of interesting questions for language testing researchers. I list a few that come to mind below.

1. What cognitive/neurobiological/socially constructed abilities/predispo-sitions/resources do language users bring to an interaction and what cognitive/neurological residue do they take away with them?
2. To what extent can we distinguish resources for interactional compe-tence (e.g., knowledge of rhetorical scripts, knowledge of register, knowl-edge of how to take turns-at-talk) from other resources that have been discussed in the literature (e.g., knowledge of grammar, lexicon, cohe-sion, rhetorical organization)?
3. To what extent and how does the effect of interaction on the language ability of L2 *learners* differ from its effect on the language use of lan-guage *users* with native-like language ability?
4. How does interaction for the purpose of acquiring a language differ from interaction for communication, socialization, acquiring, and cre-ating knowledge, etc.?
5. Chalhoub-Deville (2003) points out that "task specificity, i.e., incon-sistent performance across tasks, is well-documented in the literature" (p. 378). What is the role of variable contexts in *interactional com-petence* or *ability-in-individual-in-context*? "Where does performance inconsistency across contexts come from?"

Implications for practical test development

In my view, the most important implication for practical test development of this historical perspective on approaches to language testing is that the theoret-ical frameworks (linguistic, psychological, cognitive, affective, neurobiologi-cal, sociological, ethnographic, etc.) that researchers draw upon are typically too broad and complex to apply to all test development contexts. That is, the complexity and breadth of theoretical frameworks generally render these un-suitable for practical test development (e.g., cognitive processing models of reading for developing assessments of reading comprehension). These theories also present the testing practitioner with a specification dilemma, in that they may be underspecified in certain ways, and overspecified in others, for applica-tion to a specific language testing mandate. For this reason a given theoretical framework may apply only partially or poorly to any particular test develop-ment effort. Finally, many of the theoretical frameworks that researchers draw upon are developed within a philosophical perspective that uses falsifiability as a criterion, while for any particular language assessment, I have argued, the appropriate criteria are: 1) the cogency of the assessment use argument that informs it, and 2) the quality of the evidence that supports this argument (Bachman, 2005).

For all of the reasons above, I would propose that for purposes of prac-tical language test development we need to develop local theories, or what

Chalhoub-Deville and Tarone (1996) refer to as "operational models" (p. 11). I would suggest that an assessment use argument (AUA), such as that described by Bachman (2005), constitutes, in essence, a local or operational theory for any given test development project. Bachman (2005) describes an AUA as "the overall argument linking assessment performance to use (decisions)" (p. 16). and argues that an AUA will guide both the design and development of language assessments and validation, which he characterizes as the process of collecting evidence in support of a particular score interpretation or use. For Bachman, then, an AUA is essentially a local or operational theory that guides both the design and development of a specific assessment, and the collection of evidence in support of a specific intended use.

Consideration of the ways in which the different approaches to defining the construct have influenced practical test design, development, and use over the past half century also raises a host of questions for practitioners. At the top of this list, for me as a language testing practitioner, at least, would be a set of questions that follow from the research questions listed above. For each of these questions, the practical follow-up question would be something like, "If we knew the answer to this, would this make a difference in how we design, develop and use language assessments?" "If so, how?" "If not, why not?"

Conclusion

Issues related to language ability and language use contexts and the interaction between these have been addressed, in a dialectic, in language assessment research, and have led to three general approaches to defining the construct, or what we want to assess: (1) ability-focused, (2) task-focused, and (3) interaction-focused. While the different theoretical perspectives that underlie these approaches are not mutually exclusive, they are based on different sets of values and assumptions. These, in turn, have derived largely from the differing research *milieux* or *Zeitgeisten* in which they were formulated, the hopefully cumulative experience of the field over time, and from individual differences among researchers in their ontological stances, perspectives, and purposes, and how they define the phenomena that are the focus of their research. Because of these differences, the conundrum of ability and context and how they interact in language use and language assessment is, in my view, essentially a straw issue, theoretically, and may not be resolvable at that level.

Nevertheless, the theoretical issues raised by these different approaches have important implications and present challenging questions for both empirical research in language testing and for practical test design, development, and use. These theoretical issues also provide valuable insights into how we can enrich the ways in which we conceptualize what we assess and how we go about assessing it. For research, they imply the need for a much broader, more catholic methodological approach, involving both so-called quantitative and qualitative perspectives and methodologies. For practice, they imply that *exclusive* focus on any one of these approaches (ability, task, interaction), to the exclusion of the others, will lead to potential weaknesses in the assessment itself, or to limitations on the uses for which the assessment is appropriate. This means that we need to address all three in the design, development, and use of language assessments.

Notes

[1] Although Carroll (1973) discussed several "persistent problems" that he believed would "continue to exist and to challenge our best efforts," he touched on this particular problem only peripherally in his discussions of problems of "validity and realism" and of "scope."

[2] In this paper, I will focus on research and theory in language testing since the early 1960s. For discussions that take both longer and broader historical perspectives on language testing, see Barnwell (1996) and Spolsky (1995).

[3] See Deville and Chalhoub-Deville (2005) for an excellent historical overview of these approaches, from a slightly different perspective.

[4] Another perspective is that of Spolsky's (1978) well-known three trends or approaches: pre-scientific, psychometric-structuralist and integrative-sociolinguistic. Spolsky (1995) takes a different perspective, viewing language testing in the broad context of historical developments in large-scale institution testing, particularly from the mid-1940s onward, with focus on the development of the TOEFL and the Cambridge EFL tests.

[5] McNamara (1996) and Skehan (1998) characterize this differently, as a distinction between "construct-based" and "task-based" approaches to language assessment. However, it seems to me that the critical issue is how we define the construct to be assessed — as ability or as task.

[6] A variety of terms have been used by different authors for this general approach to assessment. Although McNamara (1996) uses the term *performance assessment*, he does characterize earlier work in performance assessment (e.g., Clark, 1972) as a task-centred approach. Skehan (1998) uses the term *performance testing*, but discusses ways of testing task-based performance in terms of a processing or task-based approach, which he appears to use more or less synonymously. Brindley (1994) uses the term *task-centered*. The University of Hawai'i group (e.g., Brown *et al.*, 2002; Norris *et al.*, 1998) appear to consider task-based assessment as an approach to performance assessment, while Brown *et al.* (2002) use the term *task-based performance assessment*.

[7] These were originally published as the *ACTFL Proficiency Guidelines* (1983) and revised in 1985. They are currently available on the Web at:

> www.sil.org/lingualinks/LANGUAGELEARNING/
>   OtherResources/ACTFLProficiencyGuidelines/
>   contents.htm

The most recent versions of the guidelines for speaking and writing can be downloaded from www.actfl.org/i4a/pages/index.cfm?pageid=3318.

4   ASSESSING ACADEMIC ENGLISH LANGUAGE PROFICIENCY: 40+ YEARS OF U.K. LANGUAGE TESTS

Alan Davies
University of Edinburgh

Abstract

The paper offers an explanatory account of the progress of academic language proficiency testing in the U.K. (and later Australia) from the British Council's English Proficiency Test Battery (EPTB) through the revolutionary English Language Testing Service (ELTS) to the present compromise of the International English Language Testing System (IELTS). The three stages of academic language testing in the U.K. over the last 50 years move from grammar through real life to features of language use. At the same time, comparison of predictive validities suggests that all three measures account for very similar shares of the variance (about 10%) and that therefore the choice of an academic language proficiency test is determined only in part by predictive validity: other factors, such as test delivery, test renewal in response to fashion, research and impact on stakeholders, and assessment of all four language skills, are also important. Implications are drawn for our understanding of academic language proficiency.

Introduction

In this paper we trace the development of academic English language proficiency testing in the U.K. since the 1950s, paying particular attention to three tests, the English Proficiency Test Battery (EPTB, 1964), the English Language Testing Service test (ELTS, 1980) and the International English Language Testing System (IELTS, 1989). It is suggested that these tests embody changing views (or paradigms) of language. We explain these changes as showing, first, a strong influence of the communicative competence construct in the move from EPTB to ELTS and, as doubts about the meaning and use of communicative competence grew, a fall back towards a compromise position (which we see in IELTS). A convincing argument for this reversal was the similarity of variance across each of the tests and a common predictor of academic success, such as end-of-year degree or diploma examination results. An equally convincing argument was the growing acceptance that test delivery requirements should be included within the scope of a wider understanding of validity (Messick, 1989). Within the tradition described in this paper, tests of academic language proficiency are seen as primarily assessing skilled literacy, the literacy of the educated, based on the construct of there being a general language factor

73

relevant to all those entering higher education whatever specialist subjects they will be studying.

Over the years, much of my work in language testing has concerned language proficiency, especially the proficiency of foreign/international students entering higher education in English-speaking countries. In the early 1960s, when I was a post-graduate student in the University of Birmingham, I was offered an appointment on a project set up to investigate English proficiency on behalf of the British Council. The project intrigued me and without much regret I abandoned the research I was conducting into Anglophone negritude and spent the following two years developing an English proficiency test, which was given the name English Proficiency Test Battery (EPTB). In due course this test was put into operation by the British Council, at first targeting their own scholars and Fellows but over time used more widely by British universities and other post-secondary institutions. The advantage for these institutions was that the test would be conducted by the British Council in a student's home country and the result used as part of the selection and admissions procedure. Furthermore, the students themselves bore the costs. British universities were well served by the procedure, which continued in use until 1980.

Academic Language

Before describing the U.K. experience of testing academic language proficiency, it will be helpful to consider views of academic language. While academic language is taken for granted as a construct, attempts to describe it as a single domain raise even greater doubts than those which query the unitary nature of academia. Do science, music, the humanities, engineering, and dentistry all share some idea of knowledge and investigation or do we just assume they do because they are all studied and researched in universities? And for us, the harder question: do they all have a language in common which is different from other language uses?

Logic (Ravelli and Ellis, 2004), literacies (Zamel and Spack, 1998), language functions (Chamot and O'Malley, 1994), range (Short, 1994), intertextuality (i.e., Gibbons, 1998), specialized vocabulary common across academic disciplines (Cunningham and Moore, 1993)—these have all been considered in the search for an explanation of the nature of academic language. Bailey and Butler (2004, p. 186) conclude that "academic language . . . implies ability . . . to express knowledge by using recognisable verbal and written academic formats." "Moreover," they say, "academic language use is often decontextualised whereby students do not receive aid from the immediate environment to construct meaning" (p. 186). They suggest that the "development of test specifications that focus on both oral and written academic language will serve the long-term goal of developing a test framework that is based on empirical data culminating in academic language proficiency prototypes" (p. 189). Van Lier

(2004, p. 161) agrees: "In terms of academic development, learners need to be able to talk about the concepts required with their teacher and peers, to participate in conversations about the issues before they can be expected to apply the concepts and the modes of reasoning in literate products." And he warns that "narrow test-based accountability cultures cut off (for lack of time, since test preparation is of the essence) the very means by which academic success is established. … Of course, in the short term, students may achieve good test scores, but in the long run, they will end up unprepared for the challenges that they will face in their professional life" (p. 161).

Academic corpora have been analyzed to show a common academic vocabulary. Coxhead (1998, p. 159), researching a corpus of academic texts containing 3,500,000 running words, extracted "a compilation of 570 word families which occurred with wide range and high frequency." However, the use of the same lexeme in different academic contexts does not necessarily mean that they always have the same meaning: "vocabulary which is characteristic of a particular context of use cannot be identified just by looking for unusual and distinctive terms, because words from a general or a sub-technical list may have technical meanings that justify including them in a specific list as well" (Flowerdew, 1993, p. 236).

There is some consensus in the notion of an integrated set of language skills required to socialize students into the acqusition of academic language: "writing … is not … a stand-alone skill but part of the whole process of text response and creation; when students use both reading and writing in crucial ways, they can become a part of the academic conversation—they signal their reponse to academic ideas and invite others to respond to their ideas in turn" (Hamp-Lyons and Kroll, 1997, p. 19).

Testing Academic Language Proficiency: The U.K. Experience

The construction and development of the English Proficiency Test Battery (EPTB), referred to above, is recalled in some detail in a volume in the Cambridge series *Studies in Language Testing* (Davies, 2007), in which I look back at the developments in academic English language testing in the U.K. (and more recently in Australia), developments that were not paralleled by the similar activity in the USA, no doubt because its strong tradition of psychometric reliability put a premium on test improvement rather than test change. While the U.K. revised and rewrote its test materials, on the basis both of principle and fashion over the 40-year period, in the USA, the Test of English as a Foreign Language (TOEFL) has (until very recently) remained as steady and unchanging as the northern star. I do not here examine other situations in detail. The North American experience has been discussed by Spolsky (1995; see also Enright, Grabe, Koda, Mosenthal, Mulcahy-Ernt, and Schedl, 2000; Davidson and Cho, 2001; and Snow, 2005). Brindley and Ross (2001) and Hyland (2004) examine other situations. What I try to do in this chapter is to explain why the British proficiency tests seemed to change so radically. Very recently TOEFL itself has changed dramatically. As well as employing a Web-based delivery, it has focused on English for Academic Purposes. It may be thought that this change has been influenced by the IELTS example, but the general shift in the climate of opinion regarding proficiency in higher education has also made itself felt (Douglas, 2000). TOEFL iBT describes itself thus:[†]

> The TOEFL Internet-based test emphasizes integrated skills and measures all four language skills, including speaking. The content on the test is authentic, and the language is consistent with that used in everyday, real academic settings. The test has four sections:
>
> - Reading measures the ability to understand academic reading matter.
> - Listening measures the ability to understand English as it is used in colleges and universities.
> - Speaking measures the ability to speak English.
> - Writing measures the ability to write in a way that is appropriate for college and university course work.
>
> Test content is based on a "corpus," or database, of spoken and written language that currently contains more than 2.7 million words, collected from educational institutions throughout the United States. (graduateshotline, 2006)

Sampling

The main problem facing a language test constructor is what to sample. If the domain under test is, let us say, ten vocabulary items, then it would certainly be possible to test the entire domain, the whole population that the test is targeting. But in the case of the kinds of proficiency tests where the domain consists of large areas of the language, it is just not possible to test everything. And so the test constructor must sample the domain and face up to the question of how to make rational choices. Should he/she select vocabulary items, and if so which ones; the grammar, again which parts; relevant texts, again which? And so on. Indeed, the only domain that could be completely covered for proficiency testing might be the phonology, but there again, the tester would have to choose which version of the phonology, which accent, which phonetic realizations.

Sampling is inescapable: that is the first of the problems. The second is related. It is what the sample eventually chosen is a sample of. That is to say, while the choice may be to sample linguistic features or forms, the tester still needs to be convinced that those features and forms have a connection (which

---

[†][Ed. note: See also Cohen, Chapter 5, for a description of TOEFL iBT.]

may, of course, be indirect) with the kinds of uses of the language that success-ful candidates will be capable of. In other words, does the language sample for the test match the criterion?

Such an approach necessarily takes account of argument-based approaches to validity (Kane, 1992): since the interpretive construct for a test involves an argument leading from the scores to score-based decisions, it follows that the language sample for the test acts itself as a corroboration of the interpretive construct.

Over the past 50 years there have been three significant attempts in the U.K. to develop a measure of academic English proficiency: they take up quite different positions on this sampling issue. The first attempt, the En-glish Proficiency Test Battery (EPTB), took a structural approach, sampling grammar and lexis (Davies, 1965). The second, the English Language Testing Service (ELTS), took a strong communicative approach, assuming that pro-ficiency has to be represented by "real-life" examples of specific language uses (Carroll, 1980). And the third, the International English Language Testing System (first and second IELTS), eventually took a more abstract view of com-municative competence, sampling what has been called communicative ability (Clapham, 1996).

All three attempts made claims on construct validity, EPTB supported by a structural model, ELTS by a communicative competence model and IELTS by a Bachman interactional authenticity (IA) rather than a real life (RL) authenticity model (Bachman, 1990). IA provides the rationale for determining the most appropriate combination of test method characteristics, thereby offering the compromise we find in IELTS between the claimed spontaneity (or *real life*) of ELTS and the structural generality of EPTB.

The story we can narrate begins in the late 1950s in the heyday of the structuralist approach to language. We note that although the communicative movement was already underway in the 1960s, the inevitable institutional lag meant that the EPTB continued to be used as the main British Council (and therefore U.K.) measure until the end of the 1970s.

The communicative revolution eventually swept all before it, first in lan-guage teaching and then in language testing (where it is well to note it was less widespread). In proficiency testing the outcome was the ELTS, which was launched by the British Council and eventually operated jointly with UCLES, the University of Cambridge Local Examinations Syndicate. This test domi-nated U.K. English language proficiency testing until the end of the 1980s. (It is also worthy of note that, as far as we are aware, no comparable test was developed for any other language).

The revolution had eventually, like all revolutions, to be hauled back, and from about 1990 ELTS gave way to the IELTS, which borrowed a great deal from ELTS but simplified its structure (even more so after 1995, when IELTS was revised), and greatly improved the delivery, analysis, and production of the test. And if number of candidates is a measure of a test's success, then IELTS has been very successful, with a tenfold increase in the ten-year period up to 2003, when there were more than 500,000 candidates. Below, we ask whether it can survive that amount of success and still remain an acceptable test of communicative ability.

We have also suggested that the explanation for these changes has to do with the view we take of language: it is that view that provides our construct and determines the sampling we employ. In the first period of our history, language was basically seen to be grammar: that eventually came to be regarded as too distant, too abstract. In the second period, language was reckoned to be a set of real-life encounters and experiences and tasks, a view that took "real-life" testing so seriously that it lost both objectivity and generality. In the third period, there has been a compromise between these two positions, where language is viewed as being about communication but in order to make contact with that communication it is considered necessary to employ some kind of distancing from the mush of general goings on that make up our daily life in language.

We can propose two alternative explanations for this development.

Explanation A

During the first (EPTB) period, the pre-ELTS period, from about 1960 to about 1980 (see Table 4.1), language was seen to be structure and hence in the test(s) grammar was given a central role. Lado's advice to "test the problems" was the slogan and so tests concentrated on the component parts of the language, parts such as phonology, stress and intonation, grammar, and so on (Lado, 1961).

The receptive skills were prominent (reading and listening), with reading dominating. After all, language teaching was still under the influence of the classical languages and hence the purpose of all language teaching, including EFL and modern languages, was seen to be to ensure that learners became literate. The model was very much that of the classical languages, but it was also (perhaps itself a spin-off from Latin and Greek) influenced by the teaching of the mother tongue, which again was heavily into literacy, genres, and textual registers. Speaking was sometimes tested, but not in the EPTB; writing was also not included in the EPTB. Indeed, the policy in TOEFL, the contemporary of EPTB, was that both writing and speaking were optional and could be tested in the Test of Spoken English (TSE) and the Test of Written English (TWE) if desired. The TSE, which took 20 minutes to administer individually, came into operation in 1979. The TWE, which began in 1986, took 30 minutes. Over time it became clear that this TOEFL model, with optional speaking and writing components, was no longer considered authentic in terms of the

Table 4.1: English Proficiency Test Battery (EPTB), in operation from 1965 to 1980

Test	Duration	To test	No. of items	Test Contents
1. Phonemes in isolation	LV/SV[1] 12 mins.	perception	65	phoemic discrimination (triplets)
2. Phonemes in context	LV 6 mins.	perception	25	sentences offering phonemic contrasts
3. Intonation and Stress	LV/SV 20 mins.	perception	50	offering intonation and stress cues in conversation
4. Listening Comprehension	LV 18 mins.	understanding of spoken academic texts		items offering 3 texts: general, science, and non-science
5. Grammar	LV/SV 15 mins.	knowledge	50	multiple choice; testing knowledge of syntax
6. Reading speed	LV/SV 10 mins.	reading comprehension and speed	196	using cloze elide items inserted into a 1500-word text
7. Reading Comprehension	LV/SV 15 mins.	understanding of written academic texts	50	using modified cloze; 3 texts: general, science, non-science

Notes:

1. LV = Long Version; SV = Short Version.
2. It was established by regression that the variance shared with criteria would be only minimally reduced if a shorter version of the test was available. The table indicates which sub-tests were presented as forming the Short Version. Given the saving in time and expenses, it is not surprising that the Long Version was rarely if ever used in EPTB testing diets.

growing orthodoxy of the communicative competence approach, which put a heavy premium on real-life language use. EPTB, on the other hand, appeared to be operating at a more abstract level, attempting to assess control over systems and structures rather than real-life language use. It seemed to be too distant from the acts and experiences of communication that we engage in every day and for which teaching (and testing) of the component parts do not seem to prepare us. It was thought to be too remote.

In the second period (the 1980s), the English Language Testing Service (ELTS), which had replaced EPTB, emphasized so-called *real-life* language use (see Table 4.2). Language was seen to be purposeful: hence the field-specific orientation of the test, built on what was called English for Specific Purposes, a cult concept in the communicative language teaching materials of the time.

Table 4.2: English Language Testing Service (ELTS) test,
in operation from 1980 to 1990

Choice of 6 Modules covering 5 broad areas of study plus one non-specific area:	
Life Science	Technology
Social Studies	Medicine
Physical Sciences	General Academic

The test consisted of 5 elements:

General tests:	Modular tests:
G1: Reading: 40 items in 40 mins.	M1: Study skills: 40 items in 55 mins.
G2: Listening: 35 items in 35 mins.	M2: Writing: 2 pieces of work in 40 mins.
	M3: Interview: up to 10 mins.

Notes:

1. G1, G2, and M1 were multiple-choice.
2. For the modular tests (M1–M3) the candidate was given the relevant source Booklet (one of the 6 options), which contained extracts, including bibliography and index from appropriate academic texts. The correct responses to all items in M1 were found in the source Booklet; the tasks in M2 were derived from the Source Booklet and the core of M3 was discussion of material in the Source Booklet.

If the rallying cry for EPTB was "test the problems," for ELTS it was "test the purposes." To that end, ELTS offered a set of modular choices, based on what were thought to be the main academic divisions. However, the appeal to real life revealed itself as all mouth and no trousers. This was especially the case for language assessment. With language teaching it may have been less of a problem because the teacher was always there to provide the necessary context and explain the cultural references. This was not the case for language testing.

If EPTB had been too distant, ELTS was too close for comfort. All intervention (and this includes both teaching and testing) involves some degree of abstraction: it is never real life simply because real life is fugitive and too full of noise. And a sample of real life is not really representative of all other possible encounters, which is why sampling real life is so difficult; we might think impossible.

IELTS (see Table 4.3), increasingly dominant in the third phase (from 1989 to 1995 for the first IELTS and then post-1995 for the revised IELTS, the current model), offered a clever compromise between the EPTB's testing of the component parts and the ELTS's field and purpose testing by its approach to testing communicative ability (or abilities).

IELTS exploits neither features of language (as EPTB did) nor instances of language use (like ELTS). Instead it brings them together by aiming at features of language use. Therefore it quite deliberately eschews any claim to specificity because what it wishes to claim is that the test is generic, potentially

Table 4.3: International English Language Testing Service (IELTS) test, in operation since 1989

1989 Version

Modular tests:
   Module A: Physical Science and Technology
   Module B: Life and Medical Science
   Module C: Business Studies and Social Sciences

Four elements:
   Reading: Module A, B, or C or the General (non-specific) test
   Writing: Module A, B, or C or the General (non-specific) test
   Listening: Non-specialized module: two tasks: 60 mins.
   Speaking: Non-specialized module: 10–15 mins.

1995 Version

The three specific modules were reduced to one Academic Reading and one Academic Writing Module: the reading and writing modules were no longer linked (as they had been in the 1989 version). The General Module became General Training for reading and writing and was deliberately made less academic.

Reading: 3 tests: 60 mins.
Writing: 2 tasks: 60 mins.
Modules (including General Training): 60 mins. each
Speaking: 10–15 mins.

---

generalizable to any type of academic language use. The emphasis has been on tasks and on production. As with ELTS, one of the great selling points has been the obligatory test of speaking. There lies the heart of the communicative aspect of IELTS and it is in speaking tests that the real break is made with the structural tradition. No longer is the rallying cry: test the problems (EPTB) or test the purposes (ELTS). With IELTS it is "test the interactions." IELTS represents a kind of regression to the mean, a (good) compromise between the extremes of the structural and the communicative.

Explanation B

There is another, more complex, explanation of the development.

While grammar was certainly central to the EPTB, the test did in fact take up a somewhat elementary approach to work sampling. The construct included a linguistic component (grammar, phonology, intonation, and stress) and a work sample component (reading comprehension, reading speed, listening comprehension): the first sampled what language is (as understood in the 1960s), the second what language is used for. As has been pointed out, the approach was wholly receptive (only listening and reading): no attempt was made to sample the productive skills of speaking and writing. In the first version (the long version) of the test there were alternative sub-tests of (a) scientific and (b) humanities texts. This choice was removed from the shorter operational version, largely because the work samples were redundant for predictive purposes. Grammar, along with reading comprehension, was central.

ELTS too was not nearly as pure a representative of the model it promoted since, as well as the field-specific modules it provided, there was also the core test of reading comprehension. Indeed, the prediction delivered by this test of reading comprehension on its own was more or less equivalent to that provided by the entire ELTS battery. What was being predicted was what at the time, in the 1970s and 1980s, was regarded as the criterion of success in higher education, the results at the end of the year examination in the student's academic discipline(s). Since language proficiency was one component only of the students' academic performance, Pearson correlations of the order of 0.4 between the test and a criterion indicative of academic success were regarded as important (see below). To that extent, and from a statistical point of view, the field-specific modules were redundant. However, since a monolithic test of grammar or reading comprehension has, it might be claimed, poor impact on language teaching, the modular apparatus was necessary to ensure good washback.

IELTS moved on from ELTS but not very far. The content of the two tests was similar — the major difference (especially after 1995) was that there were no longer field-specific modules — unless we accept that the Academic Module is specific to academia. And again, in that specificity, what dominates is the reading module. Evidence for matching to academic success is sparse but what there is suggests that, as with both EPTB and ELTS, the IELTS predictive validity correlation with performance at end of year degree/diploma examinations is about 0.3–0.4. In other words, all three tests do a very similar job, in spite of the changes in paradigm, the move back and forth between structural and communicative, and the inclusion of specific purposes testing. Nothing much has changed at the base. The variance shared by all three tests and academic success is still around 10–15%. The normal method for assessing the predictive validity of these proficiency tests was by simple correlation (product moment) between the test (usually taken at the start of the academic year) and the degree or diploma examination taken at the end of the same academic year. The only constant for all those tested was the English language proficiency test, since the subjects students were studying and therefore the examinations they were sitting ranged widely across the whole gamut of academic disciplines. No doubt this helps explain why the shared variance was typically 10–15%. While this is clearly not large, it is probably as large as one might reasonably expect, given the criterion variable used. After all, other factors such as intelligence, academic knowledge and ability, attitude, and health contribute to academic success. Language is necessary but not a sufficient determinant. If it were so, then native speakers of English would always succeed in academic programs in English medium. Clearly they do not.

Does this then mean that there is no way of choosing among the three tests?

Best Test?

The EPTB and the ELTS were both good tests, both set out to test proficiency in English for academic study, and, although their approaches are (or seem to be) quite different, they both have had much the same degree of success. However, from today's standpoint, both are out of fashion and for the sake of stakeholders, there is much to be said for keeping up with the fashion. They both had very poor delivery, largely because they were produced and delivered (and administered) as part-time activities, the first by a university department, the second by the British Council. There was no program in either case for the production of new versions, and as candidate numbers increased, it became more and more necessary to ensure proper procedures for administration, analysis, and training. EPTB and ELTS were largely one-off operations, they were not maintained with new material on a regular basis, and they did not have the advantage of being informed by new (and ongoing) research. ELTS, unlike EPTB, did test all four skills, it is true, but here again we meet the problem of maintenance: there was no proper professional training program. And they both had weak impact — or, if they had more, that was never known since there was no project in place to check.

IELTS is an improvement in all these features. True, its predictive validity (on the little evidence we have) is much the same as the two other tests. But in all the other aspects it is a superior product. Its communicative ability model is now fashionable. Its delivery (even now with the extra imposition of fixed date testing) is impressive. It is well maintained and research-led. It tests, very deliberately, all four skills. And it has ensured from the mid-1990s that its impact is monitored and the information from that project acted on. Its partnership status is also new and important. It is no longer just a British (or just a British Council) test. The partnership between the University of Cambridge Local Examinations Syndicate (UCLES), now more properly known as Cambridge ESOL, and the Australian International Development Programme (IDP) and of both with the British Council has been generally positive and now, it seems, no partner would consider going it alone or separating off. I suppose the question is whether there are other possible partners that might join, New Zealand and South Africa, perhaps. And then there may be the question of whether a World Englishes community (Singapore, Hong Kong, India) might be interested in sharing. Such a development would be innovative, given that it would mean a move away from the anglophone inner circle hegemony. But it would speak well to those who still view the British (and the English language) as wishing to continue imperialism by other means.

What the tenfold increase in candidature for IELTS over the ten year period up to 2003 (from under 50,000 to over 5,000,000) suggests is that the test has been successful. This success calls both for rejoicing and for vigilance. Rejoicing, because it demonstrates that virtue does indeed reside in minute particulars, that paying very close attention to details does pay off over time to produce a successful testing operation. But vigilance is also called for, particularly with regard to the increasing uses to which IELTS is put. Its very flexibility could cause it to lose its niche audiences and dedicated stakeholders. Furthermore, from a professional testing point of view, two crucial issues need early attention. The first is the relation between the Academic and the General Training modules. In our view, a decision needs to be taken as to whether they should be far more clearly distinguished from one another or whether they should be combined and outcomes determined on the basis of differential cut-offs. The second issue has to do with the continuing unease about the reliability of both the Speaking and the Writing components. Cambridge ESOL have made serious attempts to develop procedures that will assure stakeholders that IELTS Speaking and Writing are reliable measures, but it does seem that the doubts will continue as long as single marking is retained.

Nevertheless, we may conclude that for prediction alone, grammar, however tested, is good: hence our choice of a test of academic language proficiency would be the EPTB (perhaps brought up to date in terms of content). For face validity in academia (especially with subject specialists), an ESP approach is good: hence ELTS. And for general appeal, we would favour IELTS. But we should be aware that our combining sub-tests or modules together does not of itself add to the prediction: a test of grammar would be adequate on its own.

But a language proficiency test needs to offer more than prediction and therefore it is very important not to end this section with such a reductionist statement. Prediction, we might say, is only one part of what an academic language proficiency test is for. It also needs those qualities we have listed above so that it can be welcomed with the seriousness it deserves by admissions officers, government officials, employers, and by the candidates themselves. In other words, test validity must now take account of washback or, even more widely of test impact (Hawkey, 2006).

What Is Academic Language Proficiency?

There is an irony here. The attempt to define proficiency seems to lead inevitably to aptitude since what we are concerned with in reaching for proficiency is how to predict future performance. That seems to require a measure of language aptitude, the ability to learn the language of choice effectively when needed. This is not a new idea. In the late 1960s, my work on the EPTB led me to conclude that to measure proficiency we needed an aptitude test. And so with government funding I directed a large-scale language aptitude project. Work over several years led me to the opposite conclusion, that is that the best predictor of future performance is not an array of unconnected skills and abilities assembled to measure aptitude but present performance. What the aptitude project showed, convincingly, was that the best predictor of future language performance is present language performance. And so we can define proficiency in academic English as the ability to operate successfully in the English used in the academic domain. But what does this mean? A helpful approach is that of V. Jakeman (personal communication, September 28, 2005), who considers that IELTS assesses a candidate's current ability to study in an English academic environment. In other words, it measures pre-study rather than in-study ability.

Notice how far we have come from the communicative heyday. It may be too far since we have no way of knowing how we should test every individual candidate's future ability to study in an English-medium environment. This sounds remarkably like an appeal to a language aptitude test, although what we are in fact talking about is a test of final year secondary school language use, a pre-study test, which suggests that the distinction often made between achievement and aptitude may be a distinction too far. On the principle that present achievement is a good, perhaps the best, guide to future success, then it does appear that what IELTS offers is a measure of language aptitude. But, again as we have seen, IELTS has to be more than that if it is to be and remain the test of choice.

So what is academic language proficiency? We avoid both circularity and reductionism by suggesting that academic language proficiency is the language of argument, of analysis, and of explanation and reporting, in all cases not being specific to any particular academic area.

Academic language proficiency is skilled literacy and the ability to move easily across skills. As Pope says of physical agility:

> True Ease in Writing comes from Art not Chance,
> As those move easiest who have learn'd to dance,
>
> (Pope, 1711, ll. 390–391)

In other words, it is the literacy of the educated, based on the construct of there being a general language factor relevant to all those entering higher education, whatever specialist subject(s) they will study. For all three proficiency tests discussed, the core measures, the indispensable tests, are those to do with the written language and primarily with reading.

Van Lier (2004, p. 161), as we have seen, considers that academic discourse cannot be captured in (proficiency) tests: "narrow text-based accountability cultures cut off ... the very means by which academic success is established." He may well be right—indeed he probably is right because the bar of authenticity he is demanding of a test is just too high. Tests cannot be authentically real-life: the best they can do is to simulate reality. That may be what Hyland (2004) is reaching towards:

> Writers always have choices concerning the kinds of relationships they want to establish with readers, but in practice these choices are relatively limited, constrained by interactions acknowledged by participants as having cultural and institutional legitimacy in particular disciplines and genres. We communicate effectively only when we have correctly assessed the readers' likely response, both to our message and to the interpersonal tone in which it is presented. ... For teachers, helping students to understand written texts as the acting out of a dialogue, offers a means of demystifying academic discourse. (pp. 21–22)

These relationships, these interactions, this engagement that Hyland persuasively alludes to, are no doubt central to academic discourse and their representation in even the most valid proficiency test can only be a pale shadow. But unlike academic journals, textbooks, papers, and manuals, tests cannot by their nature use academic discourse tasks, since they require, as Hyland points out, true engagement between the reader/hearer etc. and the stimulus. What tests can do is to simulate academic discourse and incorporate aspects of academic language, its vocabulary, its formal sentence structure, its logical development and its reliance on proceeding by argument. And if we are willing to forego engagement, then the imperative to develop specific purpose tests fades away, vindicating tests of general academic proficiency.

Conclusion

In this paper we have argued that the changes in academic English language proficiency testing in the U.K. over the second half of the 20th century were not random. They were driven by the paradigmatic changes in the climate of opinion about language, following closely the movement over the period from a linguistic view of language, first to a communicative competence view and then, in the 1990s, moving back to a compromise view of language as communicative ability. As such, what the current British/Australian English language proficiency test, IELTS, claims is a general and dynamic capacity to reflect control over interactions in language use rather than a structural (and static) knowledge of language (as in EPTB) or an equally static communicative competence control (as in ELTS).

SECTION III

LANGUAGE TESTING RESEARCH: POINTS OF DEPARTURE

5 THE COMING OF AGE FOR RESEARCH ON TEST-TAKING STRATEGIES

Andrew D. Cohen
University of Minnesota

Abstract

In this selective look at research on test-taking strategies over the last twenty-five years, brief mention is made of the beginnings of test-taker strategy research and then important developments in its evolution to the present are discussed, focusing on conceptual frameworks for classifying strategies, L1- and L2-related strategies, proficiency level and test-taking strategies, strategies as a function of testing method, and the appropriateness of the research methods. The review notes the valuable role that verbal report methods have played in the process of understanding what tests actually measure. The conclusion is that while test-taking strategy research has come of age over the last twenty-five years, there still remain numerous challenges ahead, such as in arriving at a more unified theory for test-taking strategies. Another challenge is to continue finding ways to make the research effort as unobtrusive as possible, while at the same time tapping the test-taking processes.

Three decades ago, L2 assessment validation research was focused for the most part on the outcomes of testing — namely, on how tests fared in terms of item performance (item difficulty and item discrimination), test reliability, the intercorrelation of subtests and the relationship between the test and other tests or criterion variables (e.g., GPA), and the effects of different test methods. What was missing was the aspect of test validation that related to respondents' behaviours in taking the tests: little was known about what they were actually doing to produce answers to questions and how it corresponded to the abilities one sought to test.

At that time there was only a small group of assessment specialists who were concerned that claims of test validity required attention as to how the respondents arrived at their answers. As formulated in early studies (see Cohen, 2000, for details), this meant paying attention to the kinds of *strategies* that respondents were drawing upon as they completed language tests — that is, the consciously selected[1] processes that the respondents used for dealing with both the language issues and the item-response demands in the test-taking tasks at hand. More precisely, the focus was on both language learner strategies (i.e., the ways that respondents operationalized their basic skills of listening, speaking, reading, and writing, as well as the related skills of vocabulary

learning, grammar, and translation), the separate set of test-management strategies (i.e., strategies for responding meaningfully to the test items and tasks),
and a likewise separate set of test-wiseness strategies (i.e., strategies for using knowledge of test formats and other peripheral information to answer test
items without going through the expected linguistic and cognitive processes).

It proved a formidable task to obtain information about what respondents
were doing without being obtrusive, while efforts to be unobtrusive often left
us in the realm of speculation. Verbal report became a primary research tool
for this endeavor, as reported in the author's article on test-taker strategies in
the first issue of *Language Testing* (Cohen, 1984). Verbal reports include data
that reflect one or more of the following types of data:

1. *Self-report*: learners' descriptions of what they do, characterized by gen-
   eralized statements, in this case, about their test-taking strategies — for
   example, "On multiple-choice items, I tend to scan the reading passage
   for possible surface matches between information in the text and that
   same information appearing in one of the alternative choices."

2. *Self-observation*: the inspection of specific, contextualized language behaviour, either introspectively, that is, within 20 seconds of the mental
   event, or retrospectively — for instance, "What I just did was to skim
   through the reading passage for possible surface matches between information in the text and that same information appearing in one of the
   alternative choices."

3. *Self-revelation*: *think aloud*, stream-of-consciousness disclosure of
   thought processes while the information is being attended to — for example, "Hmm ... I wonder if the information in one of these alternative
   choices also appears in the text."

In the intervening years, the use of verbal report to gain a better understanding of the testing process has evolved from simply describing and
codifying strategies that respondents use to respond to different item types
and testing procedures to more theoretically based, rigorous, and statistically
sophisticated research efforts. Examples include identifying learner's use of
test-taking strategies to validate testing formats and specific tests, investigating how proficiency level and other learner characteristics relate to strategy
use and test performance, and studying the impact of strategy instruction on
learners' performance on standardized tests.

In this selective look at research on test-taking strategies over the last
twenty-five years, an attempt will first be made to characterize the beginnings
of test-taker strategy research and then important developments in its evolution
to the present will be discussed, focusing on the issues studied, the research
methodology used, and the significance of the findings for the field of language testing.

Early Work on Test-Taking Strategies

The student research studies that were reviewed in the author's 1984 *Language Testing* article that constituted some of the early efforts in the field of L2 test-taking strategies were inspired by several key studies. Danish researchers had used introspection and retrospection to study the responses of high school and college EFL students to three multiple-choice test item types embedded in connected text. Students explained which alternatives they would choose and why they thought the selected alternative was the correct one (Dollerup, Glahn, and Rosenberg Hansen, 1982). Their findings that each item produced an array of strategies and that even erroneous decoding could produce the correct answer demonstrated the potential relevance of information about learner response processes to test validity. Another influential early study dealt with strategy use in responding to random and rational deletion cloze tests (Homburg and Spaan, 1981). Based on respondents' reports of strategy use and success with different random-deletion item types, a rational-deletion cloze was constructed with four item types presumed to require different strategies: recognition of parallelism across phrases, processing within a given sentence, or the use of cues beyond the sentence in either *forward* or *backward* reading, depending on the location of these cues in the mutilated passage. Success at completing blanks requiring forward reading was related to success at understanding the main idea.

The work on the C-test (Raatz and Klein-Braley, 1981) also involved efforts to interpret how respondents produced responses to deleted material. In this procedure, the second half of every other word was deleted, leaving the first and the last sentence of the passage intact. A given C-test consisted of a number of short passages (a maximum of 100 words per passage) on a variety of topics. This alternative eliminated certain problems associated with cloze, such as choice of deletion rate and starting point, representational sampling of different language elements in the passage, and the inadvertent assessment of written production as well as reading. The introduction of this measure stimulated a series of research studies using self-report and what was referred to as *logical task analysis* to determine just what the measure was assessing (see Klein-Braley and Raatz, 1984; Klein-Braley, 1985; Grotjahn, 1987).

In the review of student research at the Hebrew University of Jerusalem (Cohen, 1984), the closeness-of-fit between the tester's presumptions about what was being tested and the response processes that the test-takers reported was explored. These studies mainly involved comparison of reported strategy use with different test formats. One early study investigating test method effect in EFL reading testing by Israeli high school students (Gordon, 1987) found a relationship between proficiency and strategy use. There were four response formats: multiple-choice questions in English and in Hebrew, and open-ended questions in English and in Hebrew. A subgroup of respondents were asked to verbalize their thoughts while they sought answers to each question. Low-proficiency students were found to process information at the local (sentence/word) level, without relating isolated bits of information to the whole text. They used individual word-centred strategies such as matching alternative words to text, copying words out of the text, word-for-word translation, formulating global impressions of text content on the basis of key words or isolated lexical items in the text or in test questions. High-proficiency students were seen to comprehend the text at the global level — predicting information accurately in context and using lexical and structural knowledge to cope with linguistic difficulties. As to performance, open-ended questions in the L2 (English) were found to be the most difficult and the best discriminator between the high- and low-proficiency students, since the low-proficiency students had difficulty with them.

A final early period study that deserves mention, one of the few conducted with other languages, looked at strategies used by students taking reading comprehension tests in Hebrew (their L1) and French (their L2) (Nevo, 1989). A multiple-choice format was used to test comprehension of two reading passages each in Hebrew and French by 42 tenth graders. Students answered open-ended questions at the end of each passage to evaluate the test items, completed a checklist of introspective strategies immediately after answering each multiple-choice item, and filled out a more general questionnaire at the end of the test. A transfer of test-taking strategies from the first to second language was noted.

Since verbal report in its various manifestations has been such an important tool in describing test-taking strategies, it has also been important to fine-tune our understanding of verbal report and how to use it in data collection (Cohen, 2000). Until recently, when it would appear that verbal report has finally gained a level of credibility and acceptability, there was not only a need to respond to criticism of verbal report methods but also to make a case for more robust verbal report methods and more complete write-ups.[†]

Themes in the Test-Taking Strategy Research

Before looking further at specific areas that have received focus in recent years, let us briefly consider five important themes in test-taking strategy research, some of which date from the early studies.

[†][Ed. note: For a discussion of new approaches in Verbal Protocol Analysis (VPA), see Lazaraton and Taylor, Chapter 6.]

Conceptual Frameworks for Classifying Strategies

The first recurrent theme deals with conceptual frameworks for classifying strategies. While the model for strategies often referred to in the test-taking literature is that of O'Malley and Chamot (1990), the debate continues as to what a language learner strategy is — and by extension, what a test-taking strategy is. A recent survey of strategy experts as to what language learner strategies are yielded both consensus and continuing disagreement (Cohen, in press). For instance, it was a matter of debate as to how conscious of and attentive to their language behaviours learners need to be in order for those behaviours to be considered strategies. In addition, while there was consensus that learners deploy strategies in sequences or clusters, there was some disagreement as to the extent to which a behaviour needs to have a mental component, a goal, an action, a metacognitive component (involving planning, monitoring, and evaluation of the strategy), and a potential that its use will lead to learning in order for it to be considered a strategy. So, in essence, two contrasting views emerged, with each having its merits. On the one hand, there was the view that strategies need to be specific, small, and part of a combination of strategies related to a task; and on the other, there was the view that strategies need to be kept at a more global, flexible, and general level. Notwithstanding these differing views, there was enthusiastic agreement for the view that strategy use and effectiveness will depend on the particular learners, the learning task, and the environment.

As indicated at the outset, this review considers there to be three largely distinct sets of strategies: language learner strategies, test-management strategies, and test-wiseness strategies. Hence, in responding to a reading comprehension item, the respondents may well be drawing from their repertoire of reading strategies (e.g., "looking for markers of meaning in the passage such as definitions, examples, indicators of key ideas, guides to paragraph development" [Cohen and Upton, 2006, p. 34]), test-management strategies (e.g., "selecting options through the elimination of other options as unreasonable based on paragraph/overall passage meaning" [p. 37]) and test-wiseness strategies (e.g., "selecting the option because it appears to have a word or phrase from the passage in it — possibly a key word" [p. 37]).

L1- and L2-Related Strategies

A second theme highlighted in a number of studies relates to whether the strategies employed in L2 test-taking are specific to first-language (L1) use, common to L1 and L2 use, or more typical of L2 use. This issue has included, for example, study of how the use of L1 in L2 testing impacts the results — for example, the writing of an L2 essay on a test in the L1 first and then translating vs. writing directly in the L2. Brooks-Carson and I found that, while two-thirds of a group of intermediate L2 learners of French at the college level had their essays rated better if they were written directly in French (with only occasional mental translation from English), one-third of the group fared better if they wrote their essay in English first and then translated it into French (see Cohen and Brooks-Carson, 2001, for more details).

Proficiency Level and Test-Taking Strategies

A third theme in the literature has been that of the influence of the respondents' proficiency level on the test-taking strategies that they employ, with a focus on the frequency with which certain strategies are employed by respondents at different proficiency levels and the relative success of their use. For example, it may be expected that weaker respondents indulge more in the use of test-wiseness strategies as a way of compensating for lack of language proficiency.

Strategies as a Function of Testing Method

A fourth recurrent theme is the question of how the strategies deployed in responding to a given language assessment measure are in part a function of the testing method. For example, in the case of C-tests (where the second half of every other word is deleted, leaving the first and the last sentence of the passage intact), it has been found that response strategies predominantly involve micro-level processing. Since half the word is given, students who do not understand the macro-context have been observed to mobilize their vocabulary skills in order to fill in the appropriate discourse connector without indulging in higher-level processing (see, for example, Cohen, Segal, and Weiss Bar-Siman-Tov, 1985; Stemmer, 1991).

Appropriateness of the Research Methods

A fifth theme is that of the appropriateness of the research methodology for the study of test-taking strategies. The above description of the earlier studies alluded to some of these methodologies, especially the use of verbal report, whether obtained through interviews or other forms of face-to-face interaction, or through questionnaires, checklists, or other means. More recently, verbal report has involved technologically sophisticated approaches (such as the software application *Morae* mentioned below, TechSmith, 2004). Whereas a robust discussion of these varying methods is beyond the scope of this chapter, nonetheless it is important to point out that efforts are always being made to refine the measures. That said, some of the earlier techniques are still the most insightful.

While the prime vehicle for test-taking strategy research continues to be verbal report, there have been a few changes in procedures for conducting such verbal reports over the years in an effort to improve the reliability and validity of the results. One has been to model for the respondents the kinds of responses that are considered appropriate (see, for example, Cohen and Upton, 2006), rather than to simply let them respond however they wish, which often failed to produce enough relevant data. In addition, in the collection of think-aloud and introspective self-observational data, researchers now may intrude and ask probing questions during data collection (something they tended not to do in the past), in order to make sure, for instance, that the respondents indicate not just their rationale for selection "b" as the correct alternative in multiple-choice, but also their reasons for rejecting "a," "c," and "d." With regard to all forms of verbal report, respondents have also been asked to listen to a tape-recording or read a transcript of their verbal report session in order to complement those data with any further insights they may have (Nyhus, 1994). These innovations have helped to improve the quality of the data to a certain extent. Nonetheless, certain issues have not been resolved even to this day, such as the impact of intrusive measures on test-taking performance, or the fact that for that very reason, strategy data are usually not collected in actual high-stakes testing situations. Hence, the strategies actually used in responding to tests in high-stakes situations may differ from those identified under research conditions.

The following section deals with developments in test-taking strategy research in more recent years, in an effort to illustrate the areas of concern that researchers have focused on with regard to test-taking strategies, the kinds of test-taking strategies investigated, and the purposes for these investigations.

Research Related to Test-Taking Strategies from 1990 to 2005

The last fifteen years have seen a modest but steady increase in the number of studies dealing with test-taking strategies, with a decided increase in the number of related areas that have been included in the research focus.

These areas may be grouped according to three main emphases of test-taking strategy research: as a contribution to the validation of language tests, to investigate the relationship between respondents' language proficiency and their test-taking strategies, and to evaluate the effectiveness of strategy instruction for improving respondents' performance on high-stakes standardized tests.

Test-Taking Strategy Research for Test Validation Purposes

As Bachman (1990) pointed out, "A ... critical limitation to correlational and experimental approaches to construct validation ... is that these examine only the products of the test taking process, the test scores, and provide no means for investigating the processes of test taking themselves" (p. 269). Findings from test-taking strategy research on how learners arrive at their test responses in different contexts have increasingly been seen to provide insights for test validation, complementing those obtained by correlational and experimental means. Such research has been used in construct validation studies, providing a new source of data for convergent validation of the construct being assessed. It has also provided insight into how given test methods, formats, and item types may affect learner responses, and how these may interact with proficiency and other contextual factors.

For example, the relationship among test-taking strategies, item content, and item performance was explored in a construct validity study of a reading test used in a doctoral study on reading strategies (Anderson, 1989, 1991). The study consisted of reanalyzing the think-aloud protocols from the Anderson doctoral thesis, adding additional strategy response categories to the 47 original ones in the thesis (Anderson, Bachman, Perkins, and Cohen, 1991). A content analysis of the reading comprehension passages and questions carried out by the test designer and an analysis based on an outside taxonomy were compared with item performance data (item difficulty and discrimination). This triangulation approach to examining construct validation indicated that strategies are used differently depending on the type of question being asked. For example, the strategies of *trying to match the stem with the text* and *guessing* were reported more frequently for inference type questions than for the other question types such as direct statement or main idea. The strategy of *paraphrasing* was reported to occur more in responding to direct statement items than with inference and main idea question types. This study marked perhaps the first time that both think-aloud protocols and more commonly used types of information on test content and test performance were combined in the same study to examine the validation of the test in a convergent manner.

Other test-taking strategy studies related to test validation have dealt with the effects of various aspects of test method or format. One approach has been to investigate whether tests using the same language material but different formats are, in fact, assessing the same thing. For example, one study compared the effects of two test formats (free response and multiple-choice) on ESL learners' reading comprehension of the same expository science text with high lexical density (Tsagari, 1994). The tests were administered to 57 Greek ESL graduate students, together with a checklist of test-taking strategies and retrospective questionnaires concerning more general reading strategies. Two students also participated in a verbal report interview dealing with the tests. Results indicated that the two tests, with identical content but different formats, did not yield measures of the same trait. This result was further evidenced by the frequency with which students selected strategies from the checklist to describe their ways of processing the same items in the two formats.

Another kind of test-taking strategy research related to test method has been to investigate some aspect of a given test format. So, for example, a study was conducted to determine the impact of using authentic vs. inauthentic texts in reading tests (i.e., real-life texts vs. texts written or simplified for language learners) (Abanomey, 2002). The study investigated whether the authenticity of texts may impact the way in which examinees use test-taking strategies with multiple-choice and open-ended tests, and whether there are significant differences between examinees who are reading authentic and inauthentic texts with regard to their use of bottom-up (text-based) and top-down (knowledge-based) strategies. A group of 216 adult, male Saudi Arabian EFL students were asked to respond to questions that were multiple-choice, open-ended, or a combination of both on either authentic or inauthentic texts. While text authenticity was not found to influence the number of strategies that were utilized with authentic as opposed to inauthentic texts, it did affect the manner in which examinees used the test-taking strategies. Whereas all readers used bottom-up strategies in a similar manner in reading both authentic and inauthentic texts, those responding to questions on the inauthentic texts reported using more top-down strategies (e.g., for multiple-choice: "choosing the multiple-choice alternative through deductive reasoning"; for open-ended, "writing a general answer"). The interpretation offered was that the modifications which produced the inauthentic texts also disturbed the conventional organization which made the bottom-up strategies less effective, and called for top-down strategies that called on previous knowledge (Abanomey, 2002, pp. 194–196).

Research on test-taking strategies in test validation has also looked at what particular test methods measure. One such study looked at cloze testing, examining the processes employed by subjects in Hong Kong engaged in a multiple-choice, rational-deletion ESL discourse cloze test (Storey, 1997). Verbal report protocols were obtained from 25 female Chinese students in a teacher education course. The students, working in a language lab, provided both concurrent introspection and immediate retrospection. This approach yielded data on the reasoning that the respondents employed in selecting items to complete gaps in the cloze passage, and the strategies that they used to do so. The cloze test began as follows, with the first blank calling for a discourse marker and the second for a cohesive tie:

> Teachers are often unaware of the reasons for problem behavior exhibited by pupils in their classes, and, ____(1)____ , inadvertently respond in ways which prolong it. Insights into the motivation behind disruptive behavior could benefit ____(2)____ in practical ways.

	a	b	c	d
1.	moreover	nevertheless	as a result	thereafter
2.	such teachers	such pupils	schools	us

The findings provided a picture of the subjects' test-taking behaviour, as well as a cognitive perspective on the question of what cloze measures. It was

found that the multiple-choice cloze items from deleted discourse markers encouraged respondents to decompose the associated arguments and analyze the
rhetorical structure of the text in some depth. The items from deleted cohesive
ties were less successful in this sense, since these items could be answered
locally without reference to the macro-structure of the text, although some respondents still did deeper processing of such items.

Three recent validation studies involving TOEFL iBT[2] together illustrate
the important role strategy studies can play in test development. One of these
studies looked at test-takers' understandings of and responses to what were
referred to as Integrated Reading/Writing Tasks (as these interacted with their
English proficiency levels), and at related issues faced by raters. The tasks
in question, on the prototype LanguEdge Courseware (Educational Testing
Service, 2002) not only required comprehension of the reading text but also
synthesis, summary, and/or evaluation of its content, all considered typical
requirements of writing in academic settings. The study investigated how test-
takers at different writing proficiency levels interpreted the demands of these
integrated tasks and identified the strategies they employed in responding to
them. The study drew on verbal report data from tests taken by students in
Beijing, Hong Kong, and Melbourne (30 Mandarin, 15 Cantonese, and 15 Ko-
reans), along with verbal reports by four raters in the act of rating. Score data
and the student texts were also analyzed. The study described characteristics
of students' responses to tasks, together with their descriptions of strategies
used and raters' reactions to the student's texts. The study uncovered numerous problems with this subtest. For example, raters were found to have a major
problem identifying copied language vs. students' own wordings. Furthermore,
whereas the researchers had initially hoped to elicit detailed information on
how students went about selecting information from the reading text, or in
transforming the language of the input text into their own words, respondents
had difficulty providing accurate insights as to how they had gone about producing their texts. The results of this study along with other in-house research
apparently led to the removal of the subtest from the exam.

The second of these studies consisted of a process-oriented effort to describe the reading and test-taking strategies that test-takers used with different
item types on the Reading section of the LanguEdge Courseware (ETS, 2002)
materials developed to familiarize prospective respondents with the TOEFL iBT
(Cohen and Upton, 2006). The investigation focused on strategies used to respond to more traditional, single-selection multiple-choice formats (i.e., *basic
comprehension* and *inferencing* questions) vs. the new selected-response (multiple selection, drag-and-drop) *reading to learn* items. The latter were designed
to simulate the academic task of forming a comprehensive and coherent representation of an entire text, rather than focusing on discrete points in the text.

Thus, the study set out to determine whether the TOEFL iBT is actually measuring what it purports to measure, as revealed through verbal reports. In a test claiming to evaluate academic reading ability, it was felt that the emphasis needed to be on designing tasks calling for test-takers to actually use academic reading skills, rather than being able to rely on *test-wiseness* tricks. Verbal report data were collected from 32 students, representing four language groups (Chinese, Japanese, Korean, and Other) as they did the Reading section tasks from the LanguEdge Courseware materials. Students were randomly assigned to two of the six reading subtests, each consisting of a 600- to 700-word text with 12–13 items, and subjects' verbal reports accompanying items representing each of the ten item types were evaluated to determine strategy use.

The findings indicated that, as a whole, the Reading section of the TOEFL iBT does, in fact, call for the use of academic reading skills for passage comprehension — at least for respondents whose language proficiency was sufficiently advanced so that they not only took the test successfully but could also tell us how they did it. Nevertheless, it was also clear that subjects generally approached the TOEFL iBT reading section as a test-taking task that required that they perform reading tasks in order to complete it. Thus, working through the Reading sections of the LanguEdge test did not fully constitute an academic reading task for these respondents but rather a test-taking task with academic-like aspects to it. Two reading strategies found to be common to all subtests were: *reads a portion of the passage carefully* and *repeats, paraphrases, or translates words, phrases, or sentences (or summarizing paragraphs/passage) to aid or improve understanding*. While the respondents were found to use an array of test-taking strategies, these were primarily test-management strategies.[3] The six common test-management strategies were:

- Goes back to the question for clarification: rereads the question.

- Goes back to the question for clarification: paraphrases (or confirms) the question or task (except for *basic comprehension* — vocabulary and pronoun reference items).

- Reads the question and then reads the passage/portion to look for clues to the answer either before or while considering options (except in the case of *reading to learn* — prose summary and schematic table items).

- Considers the options and postpones consideration of the option (except for *inferencing* — insert text[4] items).

- Selects options through vocabulary, sentence, paragraph, or passage overall meaning.

- Discards options based on vocabulary, sentence, paragraph, or passage overall meaning as well as discourse structure.

In addition, the reading to learn and the inferencing items were not found to require different, more academic-like approaches to reading than the basic comprehension items. Because they now required examinees to consider words and sentences in the context of larger chunks of text and even whole passages, basic comprehension item types were found to make them reflect more academic-like tasks and elicit comparable strategies to those required by the inferencing and reading to learn tasks. It was also found that there were no significant differences across the different L1 groups (Chinese, Japanese, Korean, and Other) in terms of the use of test-taking strategies. The findings from this study on learners' test-taking strategies would ideally lead to more precise selection and refinement of item types, so that that the subtest would better approximate the construct to be tested.

Finally, an ongoing test-validation study, which has as its central focus the strategies and sources of knowledge test-takers use to respond to TOEFL iBT listening test tasks (Douglas and Hegelheimer, 2005), also illustrates an innovation in gathering test-taking strategy data. The research interest is in identifying the strategies that test-takers use to respond to the tasks on the subtest, and in identifying the linguistic and content knowledge that they use to do so. The procedures involve the use of a software application *Morae* (Tech-Smith, 2004), which allows for remotely monitoring, recording, and analyzing the data produced by users in front of a monitor, including audio recording of the verbal protocol, screen-capturing (recording everything the participants do on the computer, namely, selecting and changing answers or attempting to proceed without having completed a question), and video-capturing (recording facial expressions and note-taking behaviour).[5]

While the participants are working on the test, the researchers are able to watch what is happening on- and off-screen (e.g., when students take notes, refer to notes, or hesitate) and to insert comments for the post-completion interviews that they will conduct a few minutes after the participants have finished the verbal protocol. These interviews consist of the participant and the researcher together viewing the video- and screen-capture and talking about the comments that the researcher has inserted. This research marks a decided methodological refinement in the collection of verbal report data, allowing for a new level of precision and comprehensiveness, undoubtedly improving on the reliability of such data collection. In addition, subsequent coding of the think aloud protocols is assisted by the use of a qualitative analysis program, *NVivo* (QSR International, 2005), which allows for the insertion and then the analysis and cross-tabulation of codes reflecting categories of strategies and knowledge revealed in the verbal protocol.

While results from the study are still forthcoming, preliminary results are yielding robust descriptions of reported strategies and sources of knowledge for responding to the TOEFL iBT listening subtest. For example, the analysis has revealed four types of strategies for approaching the response task:

1. recalling elements of the test input including the instructions, the question, the input text, or a previous question;
2. working with the response options by reviewing them in order, narrowing the options to the two or three most plausible, and stopping the review of options without considering the rest when one is deemed correct;
3. making an hypothesis about the likely answer; and
4. referring to notes before reviewing options.

In addition, there were five main categories of reasons or sources of knowledge given by study participants for selecting/rejecting options and changing a response, plus a category for no reason given or discernable:

1. the option did (or did not) match elements of the listening text or the question, in terms of keywords, specific details, inferences about details, level of specificity, or not understanding an option;
2. they drew on knowledge outside the test context, from their own life experience;
3. they referred to their notes during the response process;
4. they referred to prior experience with multiple-choice tests, or to prior questions or part of a prior question as a guide to selecting a response; and
5. they resorted to a best guess when the participant was uncertain about the correct answer.

As in the Cohen and Upton (2006) study, the researchers will be interested in comparing the strategies hypothesized in the TOEFL framework document (Jamieson, Jones, Kirsch, Mosenthal, and Taylor, 2000) — namely, *locating*, *cycling*, *integrating*, and *generating* — to the strategies that tests takers report using in responding to the tasks.

The picture that emerges from these test validation studies is that the field has progressed beyond the days when tests were validated simply by statistical analysis of correct and incorrect responses. We have progressed to a point at which we are asking crucial questions about what these tests are actually measuring and taking impressive strides to determine what it actually entails for respondents to arrive at answers to language assessment measures. The results have had an impact on the tests, even to the extent whereby the results help convince test constructors to eliminate a given test, as in the case of the Lumley and Brown (2004a, 2004b) study on an innovative subtest proposed for the TOEFL iBT.

A Focus on Test-Wiseness to Validate Tests

As a complement to the more conventional approaches to test validation, there have also been several studies looking specifically at whether it is possible to arrive at correct answers on the basis of test-wiseness rather than knowledge of the language material. A major study along these lines involved the development and validation of a test of test-wiseness for ESL students (Allan, 1992). The test that was developed included stem-option cues (where matching is possible), grammatical cues (where only one alternative matches the stem grammatically), similar option (where several distractors can be eliminated because they essentially say the same thing), and item giveaway (where another item already gives away the information). There were 33 items, each having only one test-wiseness cue in it and none intended to be answerable on the basis of prior knowledge. The students were warned that they would encounter vocabulary they had not seen before and that they could still answer the questions using skill and initiative. There were three groups of students (N = 51), with one group writing a brief explanation of how they selected their answers. The fact that the mean was well above chance (18.3, whereas 8 would be chance) suggested that the respondents did not merely guess randomly and that the test was at least to some extent measuring test-wiseness.

A more recent study (Yang, 2000) investigated the impact of test-wiseness (identifying and using the cues related to absurd options, similar options, and opposite options) in taking the test (TOEFL PBT); see note 2). First, 390 Chinese TOEFL candidates responded to a modified version of Rogers and Bateson's (1991) Test of Test-Wiseness (TTW) (see Yang, 2000, pp. 58–61) and the TOEFL Practice Test B (ETS, 1995). An item analysis of the TTW results for a subsample of 40 led to the selection of 23 respondents who were considered "test-wise" and another 17 who were deemed "test-naïve." These students were asked to provide a verbal report about the strategies that they were using while responding to a series of test-wiseness-susceptible items selected from the TTW and TOEFL. It was found that 48% to 64% of the items across the Listening and Reading Comprehension subtests of the TOEFL Practice Test B were identified as susceptible to test-wiseness. It was also found that the test-wise students had a more meaningful, thoughtful, logical, and less random approach to the items than did the test-naïve students. In addition, they were more academically knowledgeable and used that knowledge to assist them in figuring out answers to questions. Finally, they extended greater effort and were more persistent in looking for test-wiseness cues, even when it involved subtle distinctions.

We need to keep performing test-wiseness studies as a means of checking whether we are giving away the answers to items more readily than we would imagine. I still remember the surprising results of a student study I reported on in my 1984 paper, where the EFL respondents received just the title of an

English passage and had to respond to multiple-choice questions about it. The more proficient students, in particular, did far too well on the items to have had it be by chance. Even some of the less proficient students almost passed the test. The items were simply too guessable.

Language Proficiency Related to Test-Taking Strategies

A growing body of literature has investigated the relationship between the proficiency level of the respondents, their reported use of strategies in test-taking, and their performance on the L2 tests. For example, Purpura (1997, 1998) had a total of 1,382 test-takers from 17 language centers in Spain, Turkey, and the Czech Republic answer an 80-item cognitive and metacognitive strategy questionnaire (based on the work of Oxford, 1990; O'Malley and Chamot, 1990; and others), then take a 70-item standardized language test. Purpura used structural equation modeling to examine the relationships between strategy use and second language test performance (SLTP) with high- and low-proficiency test-takers. Whereas the metacognitive strategy use and SLTP models were found to produce almost identical factorial structures for the two proficiency groups, the use of monitoring, self-evaluating, and self-testing served as significantly stronger indicators of metacognitive strategy use for the low-proficiency group than they did for the high-proficiency group (Purpura, 1999, p. 182). In addition, it was found that high- and low-proficiency test-takers, while often using the same strategies or clusters of strategies, experienced differing results when using them.

In further analysis of the data looking across proficiency levels, the researcher found that there was a

> continuum ranging from product-oriented to process-oriented test-takers, where the more product-oriented test-takers were seen to be able to answer questions quickly and efficiently by retrieving information from long-term memory, while the more process-oriented test-takers might be more prone to spending time trying to comprehend or remember test input, rather than simply answering the question being asked. (Purpura, 1999, p. 181)

In the appraisal of the researcher, process-oriented test-takers, regardless of their proficiency level, would be disadvantaged in timed testing situations.

A second study comparing proficiency level of respondents investigated L2 learners' test-taking strategies in taking a listening comprehension test (again based on the work of Oxford, 1990; O'Malley and Chamot, 1990; and others). Fifty-four Japanese college EFL students took an English listening test and completed a strategy questionnaire immediately after the test (Taguchi, 2001). The questionnaire, consisting of 42 Likert-scaled items and four open-ended questions, addressed the students' perceptions of listening strategies used for recovering from comprehension breakdown, compensating for non-comprehension, and reducing testing anxiety. The questionnaire also asked about the elements that caused comprehension difficulty for the students. The results of the Likert-scaled item section revealed a statistically significant difference between more-proficient and less-proficient listeners in their perceived use of top-down strategies and in their reported elements of listening difficulty, but no difference in their reported use of bottom-up strategies, repair strategies, or affective strategies. Analyses of the open-ended responses showed that proficient listeners also identified a greater range of strategies.

A third proficiency-related study was conducted in order to determine the kinds of communication strategies L2 learners use in oral interactional situations and the relationship between their use of communication strategies and their proficiency levels (Yoshida-Morise, 1998). Sample oral proficiency interviews designed by the Educational Testing Service (1982) were analyzed, focusing on the nature and number of communication strategies in the speech production of native-Japanese-speaking adult learners of English as a foreign language in Japan (N = 12). It was observed that in general the lower-proficiency respondents used more strategies and a greater variety of strategies than the higher-proficiency respondents in order to compensate for their insufficient knowledge of the target language. Nonetheless, the higher-proficiency respondents were seen to use certain strategies more, such as paraphrase, interlingual strategies, and repair strategies.

A fourth study that involved the same structural equation modeling approach used by Purpura (1997) examined the nature of text-processing strategy use and the relationships among strategy use, levels of proficiency, and levels of foreign language aptitude of Japanese university students learning English as a foreign language (Yoshizawa, 2002). The study looked at the text-processing strategies that learners reported using when they were engaged in reading or listening tasks in second language use situations, typically classrooms and testing situations. Instruments included reading and listening strategy questionnaires, the Language Aptitude Battery for the Japanese (The Psychological Corporation, 1997), and the TOEFL. Three factors emerged from the factor analysis of the test-taking strategy data:

1. comprehension and monitoring strategies,
2. compensatory strategies (translation and repair in reading, and elaboration strategies in listening), and
3. strategies related to attention and task assessment.

A fifth study relating test-taking strategies to the respondents' proficiency level involved a large-scale investigation into the relationship between use of cognitive and metacognitive strategies on an EFL reading test and success on the test (Phakiti, 2003). The study employed both quantitative and qualitative data analyses. The 384 students enrolled in a fundamental English course at a Thai university took an 85-item reading achievement test (with both multiple-choice cloze and reading comprehension questions), followed by a cognitive-metacognitive questionnaire on what they had been thinking while responding to test items. The questionnaire was similar to that of Purpura (1999), but adjusted to suit a reading test. Eight of these students (four highly successful and four unsuccessful) were selected for retrospective interviews, which also included a 10-minute reading test (a short passage and six multiple-choice questions), to help remind them how they reported thinking through issues while performing such tests. The results suggested that the use of cognitive and metacognitive strategies had a weak but positive relationship to the reading test performance, with the metacognitive strategies reportedly playing a more significant role. In addition, the highly successful test-takers reported significantly higher metacognitive strategy use than the moderately successful ones, who in turn reported higher use of these strategies than the unsuccessful test-takers. Strategy patterns that were related to success on the reading test included reading a passage by translating it into Thai to see if it made sense and making efforts to summarize the passage as a check for comprehension.

Lest the impression be left that the use of test-taking strategies tends to have a positive impact on test results, it is important to include mention of studies that have identified strategies that may be counter-productive. So, for example, a recent study by Song (2004) with 179 ESL respondents on the Michigan English Language Assessment Battery (MELAB) revealed that while strategies such as synthesizing what was learned and linking it with prior knowledge were positively related to performance, strategies such as mechanically repeating/confirming information were not. Again, in one of the earlier studies I conducted, in this case with Aphek (Cohen and Aphek, 1979), we found one learner of Hebrew on a test of reading comprehension insisted on writing out a full translation of the Hebrew passage before he was willing to answer the open-ended questions. Not so surprisingly, he did not have enough time to answer the questions. So this translation strategy had an apparent negative impact in this instance.

Strategy Instruction for Performance on High-Stakes Standardized Tests

Finally, there is a limited literature addressing the issue of strategy instruction for prospective respondents on high-stakes standardized tests such as the TOEFL and the Test of English for International Communication (TOEIC). Such strategy instruction usually includes guidance in both test-management and test-wiseness strategies. One approach, for example, is to provide a set of "should do" strategies intended to help respondents perform better on such standardized tests (Forster and Karn, 1998). The strategies presented in this document were not intended to be specific to any one section of the tests, but were intended to be applied throughout both tests. Here are just a few examples among many:

- You should not try to understand every word in a sentence; instead, you should do your best to guess the meaning of a word, and if unable to make a guess, you should skip the question. (p. 41)
- You should always be prepared to use the process of elimination to arrive at the correct answer. (p. 43)
- When considering possible answers, you must not get side-tracked by answers which are not logical inferences. (p. 44)

The existence of such documents and of institutes that provide test preparation training has also prompted studies that take a close look at the outcomes of such programs with regard to preparing students to take these standardized tests. One such study focused on the strategies used by Taiwanese students with coaching-school training when attempting a set of TOEFL reading comprehension items (Tian, 2000). Data were collected from 43 students at a coaching school in Taiwan while they did three tasks:

1. thinking aloud while attempting a set of TOEFL reading comprehension items,
2. writing down what they recalled of the passage, and
3. answering interview questions regarding their preparation for the test and their perceptions of the training received.

The verbal report data were transcribed and coded to build a taxonomy of strategies. The participants were categorized into three groups according to their scores on the set of items and then compared in their performance on the recall task, their use of strategies, and their perceptions of the coaching-school training. The taxonomy developed from these data included 42 strategies distributed in three categories — technical strategies, reasoning strategies, and self-adjustment strategies (based largely on Cohen, 1984; Sarig, 1987; Nevo, 1989).

Comparison of the high and low scorers indicated that the high scorers tended to focus on their understanding of the passages, to use the strategies taught by the coaching school only as an auxiliary to comprehension, and to stress the need to personalize these strategies. The low scorers tended to focus on word-level strategies, to use the suggested strategies as a way of circumventing comprehension, and to follow the coaching-school training mechanically. The findings from the Tian study should serve as a warning that strategy training materials may not necessarily help those who need it the most, and perhaps

106

most benefit those who least need assistance. This review would suggest that there are advantages in making sure that any materials developed are based to a large extent on empirical findings from process-oriented studies, rather than on the hunches of the test constructors and their associates. But this review would also suggest that even if the materials reflect honestly on the respondents' true behaviours, it may not be easy to pass these insights on to respondents with more limited language proficiency.

Conclusion

The following then is a recap of key insights gained from twenty-five years of research on test-taking strategies.

Test Validation

- Research on test-taking strategies can serve as a valuable tool for validating and refining notions about the test-taking process. It can help us, for example, more rigorously distinguish language learner strategies on the one hand from test-taking (test-management and test-wiseness) strategies on the other.

- Empirical research on test-taking strategies can provide valuable information about what tests are actually measuring.

- Such research can also help to determine how comparable the results from different test methods and item types are — with regard to level of difficulty, the strategies elicited, and the abilities actually assessed, depending on the characteristics of the individual respondents or cultural groups.

- Research can help to determine whether performance on a given assessment measure is reflective of L2 language behaviour in the area assessed or rather represents behaviours employed for the sake of getting through the test.

Research Methodology

- Think-alouds and retrospective verbal report through interviews or other forms of face-to-face interaction, through questionnaires, through checklists, or most recently, through technologically sophisticated approaches (e.g., the advent of the software application *Morae*), have helped us gain a better understanding of the testing process. With regard to the collection of verbal report data for listening and speaking assessment tasks, the trade-offs between think-alouds and retrospective verbal report need to be considered — i.e., the advantages of obtaining data close to the completion of the task vs. the threat of adversely influencing the performance by being too intrusive.

- It is beneficial to model for respondents the kinds of verbal report responses that are considered appropriate, and it may be necessary for researchers to ask probing questions during data collection to ensure the collection of fine-tuned test-taking strategy information and even have the respondents review their own verbal report for the sake of clarifying or complementing their responses.

- Test-taking strategy studies have provided insights concerning the retrospective verbal report and its advantages and disadvantages compared with think-alouds. I think this is particularly important, given the difficulty of obtaining think-alouds in tests of listening and speaking.

Research Findings

- Test-taking strategy studies have successfully used a variety of statistical analyses (e.g., chi-square, ANOVA, MANOVA, and structural equation modeling) to examine the relationships between strategy use and second language test performance (SLTP) with high- and low-proficiency test-takers.

- Test-taking strategy research has provided insights concerning

  - low-level vs. higher-level processing on a test;
  - the impact of using authentic vs. inauthentic texts[6] in reading tests;
  - whether the strategies employed in L2 test-taking are more typical of first-language (L1) use, common to L1 and L2 use, or more typical of L2 use;
  - the more effective strategies for success on tests as well as the less effective ones;
  - test-takers' vs. raters' understanding of and responses to integrated language tasks; and
  - the items on a test that would be susceptible to the use of test-wiseness strategies.

As this review of the literature would suggest, test-taking strategy research has at present assumed a level of respectability as a viable source of information contributing to a more comprehensive understanding of test validity. While differences in test-taking strategy frameworks have resulted in some fragmentation of efforts, there is growing consensus on the importance of metacognitive strategies in test-taking, as well as the need for more fine-tuning as to their nature. Also clear is the need for a distinction between strategies for language use vs. strategies for responding to a test, since the former generally focus on making sense out of the language material, while the latter may simply focus on getting the right answer. Researchers are increasingly aware that theory building in the area of test-taking strategies is called for if we are to develop a coherent body of knowledge.

So what possible directions can researchers take to move the debate forward at a basic conceptual level? While it was not the purpose of this chapter to refine the definitions of *strategy*, other efforts are afoot to do just that. An edited volume slated to appear in 2007 (Cohen and Macaro, in press) brought together leading international researchers in the L2 strategy field to provide an introspective and self-critical account of three decades of research on language learner strategies. The volume deals with definitions of language learner strategies and relates strategies to individual, group, and situational differences with regard to strategy use.

Aside from conceptual issues in strategy research, there is also the matter of how learner characteristics such as L2 proficiency level, task or method characteristics, and strategy use interact, and how all of these impact test performance. One issue in this regard that still seems unresolved is the directionality — that is, the extent to which test takers who adopt strategies to fit the demands of the assessment tasks perform better on the assessment (see Bachman and Cohen, 1998).

With regard to methods for investigating test-taking strategies, we have observed verbal report methods to emerge as a crucial tool in the process of understanding what tests actually measure. We have gone from a research situation where the very use of verbal report measures needed to be justified to the current situation where such measures are accepted as a matter of course, and the researchers can focus on how best to employ them. In addition, the picture is emerging that more proficient learners are better able to utilize test-taking strategies to their advantage than are the less proficient students. Sometimes the two groups of respondents may be using the same strategies, but there is a qualitative difference in how they use them. In addition, the work by Purpura would remind us that there will be differences among respondents across given proficiency levels according to the manner in which they approach the test (e.g., more process-oriented or more product-oriented). Finally, it would appear that strategy training might have a somewhat differential impact on prospective test-takers of high-stakes standardized tests, depending in part on their language proficiency as well as on a variety of other factors. The findings from Tian's (2000) study would warrant follow-up research concerning this matter.

This review has demonstrated among other things that if test constructors have the extra knowledge as to what respondents actually do to produce answers to testing tasks, they are able to perform a crucial form of validation —

i.e., verifying the extent to which this behaviour is consistent with their expectations as to what was going to be assessed.[7] A lingering question is whether the findings from such research on test-taking strategies have actually contributed in some way to making such tests more valid. In other words, are changes made consistent with the findings? This remains an open issue for further investigation: the impact of test-taking strategy research on the refinement of assessment measures. One would like to think that the research has a direct impact but test construction and revision is dependent on numerous factors aside from the results of research.

Whereas the research reported on in this review has focused primarily on test-taker strategies used to respond to formal L2 tests, the principles and methods are also relevant to language assessment more generally. For instance, in contexts where English language learners (or indeed any other language learners) are mainstreamed in public schooling, they are often assessed by teachers in the classroom. Given that L2 students often find teacher-made tests challenging, it could be beneficial to apply test-taking strategy research to such contexts of language assessment as well.

It is gratifying for those of us who have watched the field develop to note that it is now acceptable to include a process-oriented study of respondents' test-taking strategies when attempting to validate new tests, whether they are local, in-house measures, or standardized tests such as the TOEFL. So, test-taking strategy research has indeed come of age over the last twenty-five years. Yet there still remain numerous challenges ahead, such as in arriving at a more unified theory for test-taking strategies. Another challenge is to continue finding ways to make the research effort as unobtrusive as possible while at the same time tapping the test-taking processes. This is a particularly difficult task in the case of speaking tests, since respondents cannot simultaneously speak and provide verbal report on their speaking. Fortunately the world of technology continues to produce new, less intrusive means for collecting data, such as in the Douglas and Hegelheimer study of test-taking strategies on the Listening section of the TOEFL iBT. Such advances are likely to lead to further exciting developments in this valuable line of testing research. Stay tuned.

Notes

[1] In reality, the level of conscious attention in the selection of strategies can be on a continuum from high focus to some attention to just general awareness.

[2] The TOEFL Internet-based test (TOEFL) iBT) assesses all four language skills: speaking, listening, reading, and writing. In comparing the TOEFL iBT with the previous versions of the TOEFL, the new version emphasizes integrated skills and provides better information to institutions about students' ability to communicate in

an academic setting and their readiness for academic coursework than does the previous TOEFL (both the paper-based test, PBT and the computer-based test, CBT). In addition it is a longer test, taking more than four hours to complete. The TOEFL iBT has a new Speaking section, which includes independent and integrated tasks. There is no longer a Structure section. Grammar is tested on questions and tasks in each section. Lectures and conversations in the Listening section are longer, but note-taking is allowed. The Reading section has new questions that ask test takers to categorize information and fill in a chart or complete a summary. The Writing section requires keyboarding.

3 The respondents were perhaps reluctant to use test-wiseness strategies because they knew we were observing their behaviour closely.

4 Items intended to measure the respondents' ability to understand the lexical, grammatical, and logical links between successive sentences by determining where to insert a new sentence into a section of the reading that is displayed to them.

5 To interject a caveat: While the use of *Morae* software to capture test-taker activities and actions represents a major advance in data collection techniques and facilities, the extensive data collected can apparently be very complex, and consequently difficult to interpret.

6 In the case of the Abanomey (2002) study, authentic texts were defined as those that were texts not written for a language learner audience. In this context, inauthentic texts would be those written specifically for language learners, including simplification of vocabulary and grammatical structures.

7 A tangentially related issue here is the extent to which judgments by language assessment experts as to what items are testing are reliable and valid (see, for example, concerns voiced by Alderson, 1993). Having respondents describe the processes that they actually use is a way to corroborate or refute these expert predictive judgments.

6   QUALITATIVE RESEARCH METHODS IN LANGUAGE TEST DEVELOPMENT AND VALIDATION

Anne Lazaraton
University of Minnesota
and Lynda Taylor
University of Cambridge ESOL Examinations

Abstract

One of the most important methodological developments over the last fifteen years has been the introduction of qualitative research methodologies to support the design, description, and validation of language tests. Many language testers have come to recognize the limitations of traditional statistical methods for language assessment research, and have come to value these innovative methodologies as a means by which both the assessment process and product may be understood.

This chapter introduces readers to several qualitative research methods as they relate to language testing and assessment, namely: Discourse and Conversation Analysis, Observation Checklists and Verbal Protocol Analysis. It focuses specifically on some of the qualitative studies in speaking and writing assessment undertaken by Cambridge ESOL in order to illustrate how outcomes from such investigations can feed directly into operational test development and validation activity. These research methods — together with other qualitative techniques — offer language testers viable solutions for a range of validation tasks.

Introduction

In a state-of-the-art paper published in *Language Testing*, Bachman (2000) argues that the field of language testing has shown ample evidence of maturity over the last 25 years — in practical advances such as computer-based assessment, in our understanding of the many factors involved in performance testing, and in a continuing concern over ethical issues in language assessment. However, in our opinion, an equally important methodological development over the last fifteen years has been the introduction of qualitative research methodologies to design, describe, and validate language tests. That is, many language testers have come to recognize the limitations of traditional statistical methods for language assessment research, and have come to value these innovative methodologies as a means by which both the assessment process and product may be understood.

Our purpose in this chapter is to discuss several qualitative research methods as they relate to language testing and assessment, namely: Discourse and Conversation Analysis, Observation Checklists and Verbal Protocol Analysis. There are various other qualitative techniques which we cannot cover here due to space limitations; for a broader overview the interested reader is encouraged to consult Banerjee and Luoma (1997), Lumley and Brown (2005), McNamara, Hill, and May (2002) and Richards (2003).

We then go on to examine the application of qualitative methodologies in relation to the testing of speaking and writing where such methods have proved particularly fruitful over the past 10 to 15 years. Specifically, we discuss qualitative analysis as a means to gain insights into interlocutor behaviour (the *process* of *speaking* assessment), into test-taker behaviour (the *product* of *speaking* assessment) and into rater behaviour (the *process* of *writing* assessment).

Process and Outcome in Oral Assessment

An examination of the body of research on language testing suggests that it can be grouped in two main periods: pre-1990 and post-1990. The first period was defined by research that was almost entirely quantitative and outcome-based. Construct validation studies, comparisons of face-to-face vs. tape-mediated assessments and analyses of rater behaviour were undertaken largely on the FSI/OPI Oral Proficiency Interview (see Lazaraton, 2002, for a review of this literature). Leo van Lier's seminal 1989 paper on the assumed but untested relationship between oral interviews and natural conversation was to change that, by stimulating an interest in undertaking empirical research into the nature of discourse and interaction that arises in face-to-face oral assessment. Specifically, van Lier called for studies that would even go beyond detailing the oral assessment process, to inform us about the turn-by-turn sequential interaction in oral interviews and how oral test discourse is structured by the participants. Work along these lines would allow us to determine whether or not conversational processes are at work in the oral interview, and thus whether (and how) test discourse resembles non-test discourse.

Since 1989 there has been a proliferation of studies[1] analyzing aspects of the discourse and interaction in oral interview contexts. Briefly, this work includes:

- analyses of candidate behaviour and
  - proficiency level
  - interlocutor familiarity
  - the role of the L1

- analyses of interviewer behaviour and
  - the role of accommodation

- cross-cultural influences on behaviour
- features of *good interviewers*
- its effect on candidate ratings
- the effect of gender on discourse and scores

- analyses of interviewer vs. candidate behaviour and
  - their asymmetrical nature
  - how these behaviours differ in conversation

- analyses of test format
- rating scale production
- task analysis
- candidate behaviour in the pair/group oral
- analyses of rater cognition

Many studies in this area have been multidisciplinary in nature and almost all employ transcribed discourse as the basis for analysis; a few of them employ Conversation Analysis (CA), an inductive method for finding recurring patterns of talk-in-interaction and the approach with which much of our own work was undertaken. Though even a cursory overview of CA is beyond the scope of this chapter (but see Atkinson and Heritage, 1984; Pomerantz and Fehr, 1997; Schegloff, Koshik, Jacoby, and Olsher, 2002), it should be noted that CA, in its pure form, is guided by the following analytic principles:

- using authentic, recorded data which are carefully transcribed
- *unmotivated looking* at data rather than pre-stating research questions
- using the *turn* as the unit of analysis
- analyzing single cases, deviant cases and collections thereof
- disregarding ethnographic and demographic particulars of the context and participants
- eschewing the coding and quantification of data

These principles should be kept in mind in understanding the interactive discourse data presented below.

Interlocutor Speech Behaviours on Tests

Although our work on oral interviews was motivated by an inherent interest in the construction and co-construction of oral discourse, the University of Cambridge ESOL Examinations (Cambridge ESOL), whose data are reported on below, were mainly interested in using CA as a means of construct validation;

that is, evaluating the meaningfulness and the appropriateness of interpretations based on oral test scores. Validation questions of particular interest to language testing researchers include: How might the behaviour of the interlocutor impact the oral interview process? Are interlocutors consistent across interviews with different candidates? What sort of consistency is there between interviewers for any given speaking test?

To answer these questions, Cambridge ESOL made available a number of audio cassette tapes and accompanying test materials for two of their general English proficiency examinations: the Key English Test (KET) close to beginner level[†] and the Certificate in Advanced English (CAE) at upper intermediate level.[2] The audiotapes were carefully transcribed using Conversation Analysis conventions (Atkinson and Heritage, 1984; see Appendix 1) and then analyzed on a turn-by-turn basis for patterns of interest (for an in-depth description of collecting, transcribing, and analyzing such data, see Lazaraton, 2002). These analyses showed that the interlocutors *routinely* modified their speech behaviour (and thus test delivery) in what came to be seen as predictable ways. A sampling of the behaviours found are illustrated in the fragments below.

(1) *KET Tape 20, Part 1, Interlocutor E*:

IN: you are from which country.

(2) *KET Tape 21, Part 1, Interlocutor D*:

IN: what do you- um how is <u>London</u> different from the town in which you come from.

One of the most immediately apparent speech modifications made by the interlocutors in both the KET and CAE tests is the rephrasing of interview questions. In (1), this rephrasing (from "Where are you from?") results in an unembedded wh-question; in (2), the rephrasing results in an awkward, if not ungrammatical question. Interlocutors also rephrased wh-questions into "easier" yes-no questions, as in (3) and (4).

(3) *KET Tape 19, Part 1, Interlocutor Y*:

IN: tell me something about your family.=have you got any brothers or sisters?

(4) *CAE Tape 35, Part 1, Interlocutor R*:

CA: and basically we we we deals with um worlduh bank. and of course English is uh (only) (.) way to deal with this.

IN: tsk! %okay%

[†][Ed. note: These tests are linked to the levels of the CEFR. See Alderson, Chapter 2, and McNamara, Chapter 7, for other examples of the relationship between proficiency levels and the CEFR.]

CA: so it is really [(   )

5 → IN: [right. so how do you actually use

→   your English.=do you use it on the telephone? or

→ IN: [on faxes or telexes or]

CA: [no. (.) no no   ] basically reading because.

IN's question in (4) is notable for its complexity (wh- to yes-no to several or-choices added on) and for its non-necessity (that is, the candidate begins his answer at the first possible space after the first rephrasing).

When candidates seemed to be struggling to come up with a word or complete a thought, interlocutors would often supply them, as in (5) and (6).

(5) *KET Tape 24, Part 1, Interlocutor N*:

IN: and do you <u>work</u> in Trieste? or are you a student.

CA: um I am a student at the university.

IN: uh huh and what do you study.

CA: I study pedagogue pedagogue

→ IN: pedagogies

CA: yeah yeah %pedagogies%

(6) *CAE Tape 36, Part 4, Interlocutor H*:

IN: and um Sweden is having some serious environmental problems.

CA: yeah (.) yeah th- we really have that . . . so the fish and the plants? in the sea they can't .hhh! uh(hhh) [they can't breathe [now so this   ] they died

→ IN: [breathe   [breathe yeah yeah]

While the candidate in (5) has "invited" the suggestion by the interlocutor (through an attempts to produce the word), it is not immediately apparent that the candidate in (6) needed or even wanted IN's contribution of "breathe."

Interlocutors also reacted to candidate answers in various ways, as shown in (7) and (8).

(7) *KET Tape 18, Part 1, Interlocutor T*:

IN: tell me Edgard. how long have you been here. in London.=

CA: =yes three months.

→ IN: three months?=

CA: =yes

(8) *KET Tape 18, Part 1, Interlocutor T*:

     IN: .hhh and so how often do you <u>go</u> to the cinema.

     CA: .hhh the weekend.

→ IN: at the weekends.=

     CA: =%mmm%

In Fragment (7), IN repeats CA's response from line 3, perhaps as a confirmation check of understanding. Repetitions also function as embedded corrections, as in IN's turn in Fragment (8). Here, the repetition contains the missing preposition "at."

Other reactions included evaluating and commenting on responses (Fragments 9–11) and drawing conclusions for candidates (Fragments 12–13).

(9) *KET Tape 5, Part 1, Interlocutor K*:

     IN: okay uhm Arzu. where do you come from.

     CA: .hhh I come from (.) Turkey.

     IN: <u>ah</u>. and what town are you from in Turkey.

     CA: uh from Istanbul

→ IN: <u>ah</u>. %right% okay. .hhh and do you work...

(10) *CAE Tape 33, Part 1, Interlocutor M*:

     CA: and she's twenty years old? (from   )? lives: uh:: on her own? in a small flat in the north part of: uh: Italy?

→ IN: wow.

     CA: and it's uh...

(11) *CAE (KET) Tape 80, Part 1, Interlocutor F*:

     CA1: after in the winter (really) and in the summer (.8) used to: (.8) be a lifeguard (.5) on the beach. (.5)

     CA2: mmhmm

→ IN: a <u>life</u>guard!

     ??: %life[guard!%

     CA1:   [yeah: (.5) sounds good!

(12) *KET Tape 24, Part 1, Interlocutor N*:

     IN: and- and how often do you play tennis.

     CA: at home? or in Cambridge.

     IN: uhm in Cambridge heh [heh

CA: [Cambridge no

→ IN: you don't play.

CA: I don't play tennis.

(13) *CAE Tape 5, Part 1, Interlocutor F*:

IN1: … what is she like in the class

IN2: hmm hmh hmh hmh

CA: well really she she's very quiet

IN1: quiet.

CA: yeah.

→ IN: and you're noisier.

As a result of these analyses, Cambridge ESOL instituted various means for insuring greater standardization across interlocutors on their speaking tests. Measures included the introduction of an *Interlocutor Frame*, which guides examiner talk and provides test candidates with consistent interlocutor input and support, as well as the implementation of an Oral Examiner (OE) Monitoring Checklist, which is used for monitoring/evaluating examiner performance over time and highlighting training priorities (Taylor, 2005).

But interlocutor talk is only one aspect of the speaking test process that can be examined using discourse analysis (DA). The other is an analysis of candidate output, which is discussed in the next section.

Analyses of Candidate Output on Speaking Tests

Another set of Cambridge-commissioned work dealt with language output on the First Certificate in English (FCE) Speaking Test, which took place as follow-up to the FCE Revision Project, 1991–1996. However, because the focus of this research was solely on the features of candidate language, conversation analysis, which analyzes dyadic interaction, could not be used. For this research, a broader approach to discourse analysis was considered a viable option for understanding candidate speech production within the context of an oral examination.

The research question that guided these studies was: What is the relationship between the task features of the four parts on the FCE speaking test and the candidate output in terms of speech production? A corpus of live FCE data from 1996 test administrations was studied to determine if the features of speech that were predicted as output and which were to be evaluated by the rating criteria were actually produced by the candidates. The hypothesized speech functions, described in the then-current FCE materials, were used as a starting point and were modified or supplemented as the data analysis progressed.

As reported in Lazaraton and Frantz (1997), candidate output in Part 2, where candidates are required to produce a one-minute long turn based on pictures, showed the most deviation from what was actually predicted. The FCE materials hypothesized that candidates would engage in *giving information* and *expressing opinions through comparing and contrasting*. While these speech functions did occur in the data analyzed, candidates also engaged in *describing, expressing an opinion, expressing a preference, justifying* (an opinion, preference, choice, life decision), and *speculating*. In Fragment (14), the candidate spends most of her time speculating about the feelings of the people in each picture, as she was directed, but does not compare and contrast. Here is how Lazaraton and Frantz analyzed the response.

(14) *FCE 1996 — Candidate 43 Examiner 377, Part 2*:
   (Task: Couples: I'd like you to compare and contrast these pictures saying how you think the people are feeling)

   1. yeah (.2) from the first picture I can see .hhh these two (.)
   description
   2. people they: seems not can:: cannot enjoy their .hhh meal (.)
   speculation
   3. because these girl's face I think she's: um (think) I think
   justification   **speculation**
   4. she's: .hhh (.2) an- annoyed or something it's not impatient
   5. and this boy: (.2) she's also (.2) looks boring (.2) yeah I I
   speculation
   6. think they cannot enjoy the: this atmosphere maybe the: .hhh
   speculation
   7. the:: waiter is not servings them (.) so they feel so (.) bored
   8. or (.5) or maybe they have a argue or something like that (1.0)
   speculation
   9. yeah and from the second picture (.8) mmm::: this: rooms mmm:
   description
   10. looks very warm (.) and uh .hhh (.2) mmm thse two people? (.)
   11. they also canno- I think they are not talking to each other
   speculation
   12. .hhh they just (.) sit down over there and uh (.5) these
   description
   13. gentleman just smoking (.) yeah and this woman just look at her
   14. finger

These results proved useful to FCE test developers in understanding the relationship between assessment task design and candidate output. The list of 15 speech functions generated from the study also helped to inform the assessment criteria and rating scale descriptors for the FCE and other speaking tests.

Since the time of the previous study (Lazaraton and Frantz, 1997), Cambridge ESOL has developed other means to analyze the nature of candidate output in its speaking tests. One of the most promising avenues is the Observation Checklist (OC) developed by Saville (2000) and Saville and O'Sullivan (2000) and reported on in Weir and Milanovic (2003; see Appendix 2). This approach complements the use of fine-tuned transcripts as shown above, which require both expertise and a great deal of time to produce and analyze. As an instrument that can be used in real time, the OC allows for a larger number of performances to be scrutinized, thus providing more information for test development and interpretation. The features on the checklist were derived from spoken language, SLA, and the assessment literature, and can be characterized as *informational*, *interactional*, and *management of the interaction*. Based on piloting, revision, and a mapping of the checklists onto transcriptions of candidate talk, it was concluded that they were working well.

To summarize, then, discourse analysis, both in its fine-tuned CA form and its rougher functional analysis guise, is a tool that allows for a deeper understanding of the nature of talk in oral assessment contexts, which was for too long overlooked in the test validation process. As Lazaraton (2004) remarks:

> Conversation analysis has much to recommend it as a means of validating oral language tests ... Perhaps the most important contribution that CA can make ... is in the accessibility of its data and the claims based on them. That is, for many of us ... highly sophisticated statistical analyses ... are comprehensible only to those versed in those analytic procedures ... The results of CA are patently observable, even if one does not agree with the conclusions at which an analyst may arrive. As such language testers who engage in CA of test data have the potential to reach a much larger, less exclusive readership. (p. 65)

Of course, CA/DA is not without its shortcomings — theoretical, conceptual, and methodological — and has its detractors. It does require expertise, practice, and time, and its results demand sufficient space in publication outlets (often times more than is normally allowed). It is also unclear how this sort (in fact, many sorts) of qualitative research is to be judged — what are the criteria for evaluation? Clearly, this is a pressing issue for discussion, not just for language testing but for applied linguistics in general (see Lazaraton, 2003, for more on this topic).

It will be clear from the discussion so far that oral assessment is a complex business involving many different facets (e.g., task, test-taker, interlocutor, rating criteria), all of which need to be well understood by test developers if the speaking tests they design are to be valid and reliable measuring instruments.

Process and Outcome in Writing Assessment

The same is true for the assessment of writing — another type of performance assessment involving multiple "facets" that make up a complex and interactive system (for more discussion of the multi-faceted nature of performance assessment see Milanovic and Saville, 1996). We turn now in this chapter to focus on writing assessment and more specifically the contribution of qualitative methodologies to our understanding of rater behaviour.

Understanding Rater Strategies in the Assessment of L2 Writing

Specialists in writing assessment have noted how far assessment criteria may be interpreted differently by different audiences depending on factors such as background, training, attitudes, and expectations (Hamp-Lyons, 1991). This phenomenon presents a challenge for test developers because rater consistency — both within and between raters — is considered an essential feature of good quality writing assessment. Our understanding of the processes by which raters arrive at a judgment about the quality of a performance (whether written or spoken) remains partial; getting inside a rater's head in order to access and observe the judgment process is not a simple matter! However, qualitative research methods offer a range of tools for exploring what happens during the rating process.

One of the most productive methodologies is Verbal Protocol Analysis (VPA).[†] A protocol is a "verbal report," or set of utterances, collected under special conditions and constituting a body of qualitative data for detailed analysis. While discourse analysis focuses on language content and structure, VPA involves using the language content and structure to look beyond the surface representation and to make inferences about the cognitive processes underlying certain behaviours. The assumption underpinning VPA is that "information that is heeded as a task is being carried out is represented in a limited capacity short term memory, and may be reported following an instruction to either talk aloud or think aloud" (Green, 1998, p. 7). The methodology comprises a number of distinct phases, and studies that use VPA can select from a range of different procedural variations — talk aloud/think aloud; concurrent/retrospective; non-mediated/mediated (for a fuller explanation of the phases, and the advantages/disadvantages of procedural variations, see Green, 1998, or Cohen, this volume).

[†] [Ed. note: For an extensive discussion of verbal reports, see Cohen, Chapter 5.]

Table 6.1: Coding categories

Category 1: Marking behaviours — each covering a set of activities

A1	Rater's initial reaction to script — overview (e.g., *This is laid out well*)
A2	Rater comments on their approach to reading the script (subcategories i–v)
A3	Rater comments on assigning a mark to the script (subcategories i–v)
A4	Rater comments of personal nature (subcategories i–vii)
B1	Rater comments on arrangements of meaning (subcategories i–iii)
B2	Rater comments on appropriate use of language (subcategories i–v)
B3	Rater comments on technical features (subcategories i–viii)
B4	Rater comments on task realization (subcategories i–vii)

Category 2: Evaluative responses of the rater

3	positive response
2	neutral response
1	negative response
0	query

Category 3: Metacomments

This "catch-all" category covered comments made by raters on their own rating technique, and miscellaneous comments that could not easily be coded using the other codes above, e.g., "I'm having some problem deciding what to do here."

VPA has often been used in studies exploring rater strategies to address research questions such as: What approaches do raters adopt in the rating process? What features do they pay attention to? How do they use the available assessment criteria? How do they arrive at a judgment? What distinguishes 'good' raters from 'poor' raters? Do raters adjust their marking behaviour according to the level of the script? A study to explore some of these questions was conducted by Cambridge ESOL in relation to one of its proficiency tests of L2 writing at upper intermediate level (Milanovic and Saville, 1994). The study is described in some detail below to illustrate how VPA was used.

A dataset of 20 composition scripts produced by test-takers in a live administration of the Certificate in Advanced English (CAE) was selected. The writing task itself and the assessment criteria were carefully analyzed to hypothesize likely rater strategies. A group of 20 raters received pre-training and on-site training in VPA techniques and were then asked to rate the set of 20 scripts, recording their marks on a 0–5 scale and verbalizing their thoughts onto audio-cassette throughout the rating process; in other words, the main procedure adopted was "think-aloud," "concurrent," and "non-mediated" (Green, 1998, pp. 4–7). Raters were also asked to write a short retrospective report and to complete a questionnaire that would provide supplementary data for analysis. The audio-taped verbal reports were transcribed and their linguistic content reviewed impressionistically in order to develop a framework of coding categories; the aim was to identify and label groups of rater activities or processes represented within the transcripts, which would constitute a workable coding system. Three overarching coding categories emerged, each subsuming a number of main group (e.g., A1, A2, etc.) and subsidiary categories (e.g., Ai–v) as shown in Table 6.1.

Each verbal protocol transcript was then segmented into separate units, with the unit for analysis defined as a clause, phrase, sentence, or group of sentences that identify and mark a boundary; each segment therefore represented a different activity/process. An example of a segmented protocol is shown in (15).

(15) *Transcript A/01*:

001 Beginning with the note to Malcom. Dear Malcom. Thank you for your last letter. I am really sorry that this paper got everything wrong and that you have got to bear the consequences. I hope people still talk to you. Please find enclosed a copy of the letter for which you were asking. I hope it meets your expectations. I did not put too much emphasis on all facts which were wrong but I tried to stress you have not been the mugger. /

002 Not too bad this note. /

003 Dear Sirs, Your article 'Handbag Thief Caught' from Wednesday May 27 1992. I address to you referring to your paper's article mentioned above. As I read it I was quite astonished and I would like to draw your attention to some misunderstandings which occur in this article. You give the impression that it was Mr Malcom Taylor who attempted to steal the woman's handbag. This is completely wrong. It was me, a German, not an American who accompanied Mr Taylor at the evening in question. Therefore please allow me to state shortly what has really happened. Mr Taylor and I were on our way home from the cinema as we saw a young man who attempted to snatch the handbag of a woman passing by. It was me who tried to help the woman. As a result I suffered a cut to my face. Fortunately Miss Erskine has not been injured in this incident but unfortunately the thief managed to escape. Please note that Mr Taylor's reputation suffered from your incorrect report I want to kindly ask you to publish this letter to put things right. I may allow me to thank you in advance. I hope I could help you in this matter. Write soon. /

004 He says this is completely wrong, so is this! /

005 He says he suffered the cuts, that's novel, /

006 the tenses are all over the place and it's a bit heavy. /

007 Malcom's letter is better, the letter to Malcom is better than the one to the editor. I quite like some of it, /

008 'I was quite astonished', I quite like that but he gives the impression that he was the thief./

009 'You give the impression that it was Mr Malcom Taylor who attempted to steal the woman's handbag. This is completely wrong. It was me. . . .' /

010 I had to go on reading, he hasn't really done the task that he should. /

011 I would give him 2. /

Each segment of a transcribed protocol was then assigned an appropriate code (i.e., Segment 001 = A2i, 002 = A4v3); all the data were coded as objectively and unambiguously as possible, and inter-coder reliability was estimated. Segmentation and coding of the transcript data made it possible to analyze frequency counts for main group and subsidiary categories by individual rater as well as across the whole rater group. It was also possible to subdivide scripts into *high-*, *middle-*, and *low-scoring* subsets and to explore group/individual differences in rater behaviour in terms of the main group and subsidiary coding categories. Results of the analyses suggested that *better* scripts elicit from raters attention to details such as register, style, layout, and content features. However, as performance quality declines, raters focus less on these features and pay more attention to composition elements such as spelling, grammatical accuracy, task understanding, and task completion (Milanovic and Saville, 1994).

In another study of rater decision-making processes during holistic marking of writing, 16 raters rated 40 compositions from two of the Cambridge ESOL exams at intermediate (FCE) and advanced Certificate of Proviciency in English (CPE) levels (Milanovic, Saville, and Shuhong, 1996). After an initial training session, three types of data were collected from the raters: a retrospective written report (i.e., after rating each composition raters noted what had gone through their minds in reaching a judgment); a concurrent verbal report (i.e., raters audio-recorded a verbal report while rating a limited number of compositions); and a group interview (i.e., a 30-minute structured interview). Data from the audio-taped concurrent reports and group interviews were transcribed; along with the retrospective written reports, these were reviewed impressionistically to develop a suitable scheme for coding the transcripts. Analyses of the coded data resulted in findings relating to two dimensions: firstly, the broad approaches taken by raters to the process of marking, and secondly, the details of their approach, i.e., the particular composition elements raters claim to focus on and the relative weight they claim to attach to these elements.

The four broad rating approaches identified in this study were: 1) principled two-scan/read, 2) pragmatic two-scan/read, 3) read-through, and 4) provisional mark. In terms of their detailed approach, raters appeared to focus on 11 composition elements: length, legibility, grammar, structure, communicative effectiveness, tone, vocabulary, spelling, content, task realization, and punctuation.[3]

Results from VPA studies such as those we have described can play an important role in informing test developers' decisions on design of writing prompts/tasks and selection of writing assessment criteria, especially at different proficiency levels; such studies also inform and improve procedures for rater training and standardization. VPA was also used, for example, at the end of the IELTS Writing Revision Project (2001–2005) to check raters' interpretation and application of the new assessment criteria and to confirm how the revised rating scale was functioning (Falvey and Shaw, 2006).

Conclusion

It has become increasingly apparent that the established psychometric methods for test validation are effective, but limited, and other methods are required for us to gain a fuller understanding of the language tests we use. Two decades ago Cohen (1984) and Grotjahn (1986) advocated the use of introspection techniques as a means of gathering information to feed directly into the test development and validation process. Since then introspection techniques, such as verbal protocol analysis, together with other qualitative research methods, such as conversation and discourse analysis, have been increasingly used by applied linguists and language testers to explore a range of test-related issues.

We have chosen in this article to focus specifically on some of the qualitative studies in speaking and writing assessment undertaken by Cambridge ESOL in order to illustrate how outcomes from such investigations can feed directly into operational test development and validation activity. It should be noted, however, that many qualitative studies have been conducted with speaking and writing tests other than the Cambridge examinations. Conversation analysis, discourse analysis, and verbal protocol analysis — along with other qualitative research methods — now offer language testers viable solutions for these validation tasks.

Notes

[1] See Lazaraton (2002) for details on and citations for these studies.

[2] University of Cambridge ESOL Examinations is a non-teaching department of the University of Cambridge and offers language proficiency examinations in English. The general English exams referred to in this chapter are linked to the levels of the *Common European Framework of Reference* published by the Council of Europe (2001) in the following way: KET (A2), PET (B1), FCE (B2), CAE (C1) and CPE (C2).

[3] Space restrictions prevent a fuller description of these results; see Milanovic, Saville, and Shuhong, 1996, for more information.

Appendix 1

Transcription Notation Symbols

(adapted from Atkinson and Heritage, 1984, pp. ix–xvi)

1. **unfilled pauses or gaps:** periods of silence, timed in tenths of a second by count-ing "beats" of elapsed time. Micropauses, those of less than 0.2 seconds, are symbolized (.); longer pauses appear as a time within parentheses: (.5) is five tenths of a second.

2. **colon (:):** a lengthened sound or syllable; more colons prolong the stretch.

3. **dash (-):** a cut-off, usually a glottal stop.

4. **.hhh:** an inbreath; **.hhh!** — strong inhalation.

5. **hhh:** exhalation; **hhh!** — strong exhalation.

6. **hah, huh, heh, hnh:** all represent laughter, depending on the sounds produced. All can be followed by an (!), signifying stronger laughter.

7. **(hhh):** breathiness within a word.

8. **punctuation:** markers of intonation rather than clausal structure; a period (.) is falling intonation, a question mark (?) is rising intonation, a comma (,) is con-tinuing intonation. A question mark followed by a comma (?,) represents rising intonation, but is weaker than a (?). An exclamation mark (!) is animated into-nation.

9. **equal sign (=):** a latched utterance, no interval between utterances.

10. **brackets ([ ]):** overlapping talk, where utterances start and/or end simultaneously.

11. **percent signs (% %):** quiet talk.

12. **caret (^):** a marked rising shift in pitch.

13. **arrows (> <):** the talk speeds up, **arrows (< >)** — the talk slows down.

14. **psk:** a lip smack, *tch* — a tongue click.

15. **underlining or CAPS:** a <u>word</u> or SOund is emphasized.

16. **arrow (→):** a feature of interest to the analyst.

17. **empty parentheses ( ):** transcription doubt, uncertainty; words within parentheses are uncertain.

18. **double parentheses (( )):** non-vocal action, details of scene.

Appendix 2

Observation checklist for speaking test validation

(from Weir and Milanovic, 2003, p. 453)

Informational functions

Providing personal information	• give information on present circumstances • give information on past circumstances • give information on future plans
Expressing opinions	express opinions
Elaborating	elaborate on or modify an opinion
Justifying opinions	express reasons for assertions s/he has made
Comparing	compare things/people/events
Speculating	speculate
Staging	separate out or interpret the parts of an issue
Describing	• describe a sequence of events • describe a scene • describe a person
Summarising	summarise what s/he has said
Suggesting	suggest a particular idea
Expressing preferences	express preferences

Interactional functions

Agreeing	agree with an assertion made by another speaker (apart from 'yeah' or non-verbal)
Disagreeing	disagree with an assertion made by another speaker (apart from 'no' or non-verbal)
Modifying	modify arguments or comments made by another speaker or by the test-taker in response to another speaker
Asking for opinions	ask for opinions
Persuading	attempt to persuade another person
Asking for information	ask for information
Conversational repair	repair breakdowns in interaction
Negotiating meaning	• check understanding • indicate understanding of point made by partner • establish common ground/purpose or strategy • ask for clarification when an utterance is misheard or misinterpreted • correct an utterance made by another speaker which is perceived to be incorrect or inaccurate • respond to requests for clarification

Managing interaction

Initiating	start any interactions
Changing	take the opportunity to change the topic
Reciprocating	share the responsibility for developing the interaction
Deciding	come to a decision

Example of the observation checklist used to analyse functional content across the 4 parts of a paired speaking test
(Test 1 FCE, 1998-99, Candidates A and B)

	OPERATIONS		Task 1 A	Task 1 B	Task 2 A	Task 2 B	Task 3 A	Task 3 B	Task 4 A	Task 4 B
I	Providing personal information	Present	√	√	√	√	√	√	√	√
N		Past		√						
F		Future	√	√						
O	Expressing opinions		√	√	√	√	√	√	√	√
R	Elaborating		√	√	√	√	√	√	√	√
M	Justifying opinions		√		√	√	√	√	√	√
A	Comparing		√		√	√	√	√		
T	Speculating		√	√	√				√	√
I	Staging		√		√					
O	Describing		√	√	√	√				
N	Summarising									
A	Suggesting						√		√	√
L	Expressing preferences		√	√	√	√	√			
I	Agreeing						√	√	√	√
N	Disagreeing						√	√		
T	Modifying						√		√	
E	Asking for opinions						√	√		
R	Persuading						√	√		
A	Asking for information									
C	Conversational repair						√	√		
T	Negotiating meaning	Check understanding					√			
I		Indicate understanding					√	√		
O		Establish common ground								
N		Ask for clarification		√					√	
A		Correct an utterance								
L		Respond to requests for clarification								
Managing interaction	Initiating						√			
	Changing									
	Reciprocating						√	√		
	Deciding									

129

7 LANGUAGE TESTING: A QUESTION OF CONTEXT

Tim McNamara
University of Melbourne

Abstract

Arguably the greatest challenge facing language testing is the issue of the context in which language testing is carried out, both at the micro and the macro level. In standard works on language testing, context has been theorized in terms of the demands it makes on individual cognitive attributes, but this has distorted the picture of the social context available to us. The social context theorized in its own terms has featured rather weakly in discussions of language tests. At the micro level, insights from Conversation Analysis have challenged the individualistic focus of current thinking about assessment. At the macro level, the awareness of social context has led to the development of critical language testing and an understanding that language testing constructs, implicitly or explicitly, may be sociolinguistic in origin, in the context of the use of language tests as markers of identity in settings marked by inter-group conflict. The paper argues that all language tests can be seen as tests of identity in the light of the theory of subjectivity proposed by Foucault, using as an example the Occupational English Test, a test of English as a second language for immigrant health professionals. The paper concludes with an argument for a deeper engagement with contemporary social theory in language testing research.

In this retrospective paper I advocate a renewed discussion of the social context of language testing. This involves investigating the claim that all language tests are tests of identity. Such a claim is based on the reconceptualization of identity as subjectivity within recent social theory. In the discussion, I will refer to the Occupational English Test (OET) (McNamara, 1996), an Australian test of second language proficiency for immigrant health professionals.

The themes of the paper reflect the development of interests I had at the time I first attended the Language Testing Research Colloquium (LTRC), in San Francisco in 1990. At that LTRC I gave a paper reporting some of the findings of my PhD research on the validation of the OET, which I was at that time in the throes of completing. This was in fact my second PhD topic; the first, on which I had worked on and off for four years, had been a study of language and identity, but midway through I abandoned it and changed my focus to language testing, largely for pragmatic, job-related reasons. Recently, I have begun to teach again in the area of language and identity, and I have found much in that field to stimulate, challenge, and deepen my understanding of language testing as a social practice. I would like to present some of this recent thinking in this paper.

How can language tests be seen as tests of identity? How does this apply to proficiency tests such as the OET? The function of certain language tests as techniques for identification is of course recognized in the literature on language testing; for example, in the frequent references to the Biblical shibboleth test, in which a single pronunciation feature was used to detect defeated enemy soldiers trying to "pass" among the victors (Spolsky, 1995). This function is currently of great interest in the recent critical discussion of the growing use of language tests within the asylum process (Eades, Fraser, Siegel, McNamara, and Baker, 2003; Reath, 2004; Language and National Origin Group, 2004; Eades, 2005). Determining which side of a political border a person is from, sometimes on the basis of a language test, may result in the individual being granted or denied refugee status under international law. Asylum seekers are interviewed by an immigration officer either through an interpreter or through the medium of a lingua franca, and a tape recording of the interview is subjected to language analysis, on the basis of which a claim is made as to the sociolinguistic and hence national identity of the speaker (Eades, 2005). The goal of identity tests such as this, and aspects of the procedures involved, seem obviously different from the goals and procedures of language proficiency testing. However, I want to show that by rethinking the *social context* of language tests, the distinction between tests of proficiency and tests for identification disappears. All language tests are about identification.

Before developing this point further, I want to briefly consider the way in which the social context of the test is conceptualized within the standard works on proficiency testing, for example in Bachman's (1990) *Fundamental Considerations in Language Testing*. We need to distinguish context at two levels: the micro, that is, the immediate context, such as the context of performance in face-to-face speaking tests, and the macro, or wider social context. The discussion of context in Bachman (1990) focuses on the micro level. The emphasis in this discussion, a reflection of the broader traditions both of linguistics and educational measurement in which Bachman's work is firmly located, is cognitive and psychological, even if the definition of the context with which language proficiency must engage is described in part in terms made available from the ethnographic work of Dell Hymes. Context is addressed most clearly in the notion of the target language use situation, which is conceived from the perspective of the language user; this reflects a wider needs-based emphasis in communicative language teaching. The target language use situation is defined in terms of its demands on the language user; this allows the test method facets — the test content and the testing procedures — to represent the interface between the dimensions of communicative language ability and the demands of the target language use situation. In order for this set-up to work, the demands of the context are necessarily understood as cognitive demands. There is thus a feedback loop between context and ability: the target language use situation is conceptualized in terms of components of communicative language ability, which in turn is understood as ability to handle the target language use situation. The situation or context is projected onto the learner as a demand for a relevant set of cognitive abilities; in turn, these cognitive abilities are read onto the context.

What we do not have here is a theory of the social context in its own right, as it were, that is, a theory that is not primarily concerned with the cognitive demands of the setting on the candidate. In fact, a fully developed social theory of the face-to-face context does exist in the form of Conversation Analysis (CA). While this has been the basis for an increasing volume of research in language testing (Young and He, 1998; Brown, 2003, 2005; Brown and McNamara, 2004), the theoretical dilemmas involved in the use of CA in this context are far from resolved. Beyond this, the wider social context in which the immediate target use situation is located has been less well theorized. While the social implications of test use have been considered in the language testing literature at least since Spolsky (1981) and are discussed, albeit rather briefly, in Bachman (1990), discussion is restricted to the intended and unintended consequences of the test, not to the wider social meaning of the test in its context. There is a gap, in other words, in our theorizing of the social context in which language tests find their place.

Contemporary social theory offers a rich array of conceptual frameworks in terms of which one could potentially conceptualize the social context and role of language tests. One particularly relevant one, which additionally addresses the question of examinations, is in the work of Michel Foucault. Foucault addresses the way in which social identities, what he calls subject positions, become available as a function of dominant discourses ("big D" discourses, to use Pennycook's 1994 term) at any given historical moment. In his book *Discipline and Punish* (Foucault, 1977 [1975]), he sees the discourses of modernity which emerged in the late 18th and early 19th centuries as involving the instilling of a sense of self through techniques of surveillance, primary among which is the examination. In Foucault's brilliant analysis of the relationship between tests and power, he shows us how tests can be experienced as exercises in subjection to power, a process that is productive of individuality or, as he terms it, subjectivity:

> The examination as the fixing, at once ritual and 'scientific', of individual
> differences, as the pinning down of each individual in his own particularity
> ... clearly indicates the appearance of a new modality of power in which
> each individual receives as his status his own individuality, and in which

133

> he is linked by his status to the features, the measurements, the gaps, the
> 'marks' that characterize him and make him a 'case'. (p. 192)

This means that the certification we gain as a result of our subjection to processes of examination confers an identity — we become socially visible as
possessing the qualities the examination seeks to establish. We thus become
socially visible in the social roles — the subject positions — available within
the discourse. Examples of this process will be given below, in relation to the
certification of immigrant health professionals, and in the identities conferred
within policy-related assessment frameworks, which dominate contemporary
language education. Accepting such a theory of social context would bring
about significant changes in the way we think about our tests and our role
as language testers. It would impel us to envisage the testee not only as an
individual with cognitive attributes defined in terms of the theorized features
of the immediate situation of use, but as a social being whose subjectivity is
a function of subject *positions* realized in the administration and use, the very
existence, of the test itself. From this perspective, tests become technologies of
subjectivity. They act as mechanisms both for the definition of subject positions
and for the recognition of subjects. Tests create the identities they measure.

Subject positions are articulated within discourses. For example, the subjectivities defined within the discourse of modern clinical practice are the topic
of Foucault's *The Archaeology of Knowledge* (1972 [1969]). Foucault defines
clinical medicine as a discourse:

> Clinical medicine must ... be regarded as the establishment of a rela-
> tion, in medical discourse, between a number of distinct elements, some
> of which concern[ed] the status of doctors, others the institutional and
> technical site from which they sp[eak], others their position as subjects
> perceiving, observing, describing, teaching, etc. It can be said that this re-
> lation between different elements ... is effected by clinical discourse: it
> is this, as a practice, that establishes between them all a system of rela-
> tions ... (p. 50)

Foucault discusses each of the elements in the system of relations that constitutes a discourse: speaker status, site of speaking, and subject positions of
speakers. All of them are constituted in part or in whole in language. This
means that the question of who is accorded the right to speak in such a discourse, and from where, and occupying which subject position, is obviously of
crucial relevance to understanding the function of the language tests that guard
access to this right.

On the status of the speaker, Foucault writes:

> First question: who is speaking? Who ... is accorded the right to use
> this sort of language? Who is qualified to do so? Who derives from it his
> own special quality, his prestige ... ? What is the status of the individuals

who — alone — have the right ... to proffer such a discourse? ... Medical statements cannot come from anybody ... (p. 51)

The status of speaker in medical discourses is rigorously guarded; as a result, immigrant health professionals, who have gained the right to speak in their own culture, need to go through a process of recognition before that status is again conferred on them in the new cultural setting. Language examinations are a typical aspect of such processes.

Foucault goes on to consider the subject positions defined within medical discourse:

> The positions of the subject are also defined by the situation that it is possible for him to occupy ... : according to a certain grid of explicit or implicit interrogations, he is the questioning subject and, according to a certain programme of information, he is the listening subject; according to a table of characteristic features, he is the seeing subject, and, according to a descriptive type, the observing subject; ... To these perceptual situations should be added the positions that the subject can occupy in the information networks (in theoretical teaching or in hospital training; in the system of oral communication or of written document: as emitter and receiver of observations, case-histories, statistical data, general theoretical propositions, projects, and decisions). (p. 52)

These subject positions are in contemporary language testing practice the basis for the content of relevant language tests. What makes his analysis different from the job analysis stage in the development of specific purpose language tests, which it superficially resembles, is that such subjectivities are implicated in relations of power; thus Foucault's analysis is not an exercise in pragmatism but a social critique.

Foucault's notion of discourse clarifies for us the socially contextual function of a test of English for the certification of immigrant health professionals, such as the OET (McNamara, 1996). This Australian test has existed in one form or another for over 30 years, as part of the process required by the professional registration authorities for the recognition of the professional credentials of immigrant health professionals. It was reformed in the mid 1980s to reflect the communicative demands of the workplace, and now it contains assessments in the four skills of listening, speaking, reading, and writing based on tasks that are characteristic of the workplaces of the various health professionals for whom the test is designed. From a Foucauldian perspective, the function of the OET is clear: it is a technology for recognizing (that is, publicly confirming and certifying) individuals as suitable objects of such subject positions. In this sense, the OET, like other tests, is a test of identity. Like all tests, it represents a site of social recognition and control.

135

What advantages are there for us as language testing professionals seriously engaging with a theory of the social context of testing?

First, we can avoid being merely naïve players in this discursively constructed world. With appropriate intellectual and analytical tools we are enabled to become aware of the roles that tests will play in the operation of power and of systems of social control. We will be less inclined to shelter in the impersonality of the purely technical aspects of our work. We need critical self-awareness in order for us first to become aware of and then to decide whether to accept or to resist our own subject positions in the system of social control in which tests play such a part. LTRC as a conference will enable us to reflect on our subject positions — our identities — as language testers, rather than simply reinforcing them.

Second, we will be able to understand how the emphasis on the cognitive and psychological in measurement is part of the means through which the social construction of subjectivity, and hence the social function of the test, is rendered invisible. The point about subjectivity is well made by Butler (1990) in her discussion of the performative nature of gendered identity:

> If the 'cause' of desire, gesture and act can be localized within the 'self' of the actor, then the political regulatory and disciplinary practices which produce that ostensibly coherent gender are effectively displaced from view. The displacement of a political and discursive origin of gender identity onto a psychological 'core' precludes an analysis of the political constitution of the gendered subject. (p. 136)

Third, attention to social theory will help break down the isolation of language testers from areas of the humanities in which social theoretical awareness is articulated, which I see as currently one of the most vulnerable aspects of our field. Without critical awareness ourselves, we will be ill-equipped to engage with the challenges presented by our critics.

Fourth, a theorization of the social context of testing will help us understand the discourses in which the demands of our sponsors and clients are shaped. This will better prepare us to expect, to recognize, and to deal as constructively as we can with various kinds of pressures on tests as a result of their function as sites of social control. For example, the OET is subject to relatively abrupt changes in policy, both in who will be required to take it and at what level of performance permission to practice will be granted. This is because the test acts as a site for the insertion of the power of competing discourses, of government responsibility for provision of medical services in settings of scarcity of medical resources, such as in rural areas, of patients' rights, of multiculturalism, and so on. Other examples of test as sites of social control are the dictating of test constructs as a function of government policy, as in the mandating of levels on the Common European Framework of Reference for Languages (Council of Europe, 2001; Fulcher, 2004b) or the imposition of testing regimes such as the No Child Left Behind Policy (Kunnan, 2005b; Byrnes, 2005). We should also expect that those in power will want to retain control of the setting of cut scores in the interests of policy objectives. A clear example recently has been the role of language tests in current discourses on immigration and citizenship. The legislation on immigration and citizenship in several European countries makes reference to levels on the Common European Framework of Reference for Languages (Council of Europe, 2001). There are six levels, A1 and 2, B1 and 2, and C1 and 2, spanning the range of language proficiency from beginner to fluent, native-like command; A1 is the lowest level. The levels required under this legislation differ by country, depending on the politics of the setting. Austria has recently increased from A1 to A2 the language requirement that immigrants need to demonstrate within 18 months of residency, or face loss of residence rights (König and Perchinig, 2005); the Netherlands requires new migrants to reach A2 (Marinelli, 2005); Finland requires A2 for members of Finnish ethnic communities in Russia wishing to reside in Finland; recent changes to both the German and Danish citizenship laws require B1. The politics and cultural values of the setting in each case appear to be the decisive factor, as it is hard to see what justification there might be for the different levels in terms of the functional requirements of citizenship, which are presumably equivalent across countries.

Finally, engagement with the theory of the social context represents a response to one of the requirements of test validation as expressed by Messick (1989), that the values implicit in test constructs be investigated and articulated. These values can be understood in social and policy-related terms and can be revealed by considering the discourses within which language tests are located and have their meaning. The extent to which individual test developers should be required to demonstrate such a consciousness is obviously highly debatable, and here we come up against the limits of current validity theory as represented by Messick and Bachman, in that, lacking an adequate social theory, it is not adequate to deal with the perspective made available within a social theoretical orientation (McNamara and Roever, 2006). But even if test developers do not carry out the kind of research being advocated here, there is clearly a need for this research to be carried out within language testing as a research area more broadly conceived.

For all the reasons cited, theories of the social context of language testing should be the site of urgent exploration. We obviously have a long way to go if we are to develop such a tradition of addressing the social context of language tests at our conferences and in our research. But the challenge is both intellectually exciting and necessary for informing our awareness and our practice.

SECTION IV

ANTECEDENTS
AND
PROSPECTS

8 TESTS AS POWER TOOLS: LOOKING BACK, LOOKING FORWARD

Elana Shohamy
Tel Aviv University

Abstract

In this chapter I discuss current uses of language tests in education and society, arguing that tests have become primary tools used by policy makers to resolve and reform educational, political, and social problems. Specifically, I address two areas where this is happening: (1) in the realm of education, through the introduction of the No Child Left Behind tests in the USA, intended to reform education and resolve low school achievements; and (2) in the realm of society, through the increasing use of language tests for granting citizenship and thus, using tests to settle the complex set of issues related to migration. Relying on empirical research, I point to the length of time it takes immigrants to achieve academic language proficiency in schools and the continued role of L1; I argue that the use of such tests is unjust, unethical, and discriminatory and leads to marginalization and expulsion of people, suppression of diversity, and forced monolingualism. Further, these tests do not accurately represent current understanding of the language constructs of immigrants, who continue to negotiate and make meaning multilingually. I end the chapter with a call for the creation of language tests that are both in line with broader and more realistic language constructs, incorporate multilingualism, and multimodal realities, and also address the misuses of tests in order to lead to inclusion, participation, and recognition, especially given the ramifications of tests in creating de facto language policies.

Introduction

In this final chapter of *Language Testing Reconsidered*, I share my retrospection about language testing, based on my experiences in the field. In fact, this task has been instructive on a personal level as it forced me to take a hard look into my own motivations and complex relationship with language testing. Of course, I often wonder whether experience and seniority provide a sensible and creative perspective or whether they serve as devices that block and suppress thinking. Experience may provide an ability *to see*, but mostly using specific and pre-defined glasses. With this caveat in mind, I look back and offer insights from my experience, by providing my own narrative about language testing using my personal glasses, a narrative that has led me to develop a critical view of the state of the art in the field of language testing.

141

A Personal Narrative About Testing

Language testing for me, from the day I first started engaging with it, was about *reforming the world*. Being a victim of tests myself, I remembered very well my school days when tests were a hurdle, an *unpleasant* experience. It was tests that were responsible for turning the enjoyment and fun of learning into pain, tension, and a feeling of unfairness. Tests were often the source of anger, frustration, pressure, competition, and even humiliation. Coming out of tests was often accompanied by a feeling that my real knowledge could not be expressed. As a student in school, I recall often not understanding what tests were all about, why they were needed, and what their purpose was in the midst of rewarding and enjoyable learning experiences. Having to take a test often felt like betrayal. If learning is so meaningful, rewarding, and personal, why is it that it needs to be accompanied by the unpleasant events of *being tested*?

During my high school years, the testing experience was even more negative, as I was faced with *the big tests*, such as national tests at the end of high school or entrance tests to the university: it was clear that these tests could affect my whole future life. They could determine which university I would be accepted to, or whether I would be admitted to a university at all. High school was the period when tests replaced learning, as testing dominated both teaching and learning. I clearly recall how little meaningful learning took place during the last two years of high school, which were devoted almost exclusively to preparing for *the big tests*. The negative experiences of testing would spread to my home, where I was constantly being judged by my parents on the basis of my performance on the tests (often in relation to my other classmates), as if nothing else mattered. I do not remember being asked about "what I learned in school today" but rather "what grade I got on a given test." Tests became the sole criterion of success. Thinking about these issues now, I realize that students in schools rarely received any explanation of why tests were even needed, who benefited from them, and in what ways. But, as with all other school activities, students just complied. So although testing was an unpleasant experience, it was viewed as a necessary evil that was never questioned. Students were expected to conform to and accept, no questions asked, this integral part of schooling as just part of life.

Enrolling at the university for an advanced degree in language education and applied linguistics seemed to offer an excellent opportunity to delve deeply into the topic of testing, for no reason other than to better understand its mysteries, rationale, purposes, benefits, and costs. I was determined to understand the mysteries of testing and to possibly create better tests. I had a vision of tests as something different, perhaps without scores or without grades, without multiple choices that never made sense, and perhaps involving stimulating and exciting situations integrated in a productive way into learning.

Yet, when I became immersed in psychometrics, measurement, and statistics courses as requirements in graduate school, the focus was not on these types of issues. It was not about creating better tests from the experiential perspective or integrating testing with better learning, but rather it was all about formulas. It was understood that better tests would be achieved only if they became more reliable and valid by using sophisticated formulas and calculations, but there was nothing about *the testing experience*. In order to survive in graduate school, it was necessary to pass a large number of tests in all these measurement courses, similar to the types of tests administered in high school. Again, one had no choice but to comply: passing tests was clearly a demand in the field of testing, consisting at the time almost exclusively of men who knew math and statistics. These courses had little to do with real tests, with real people, or with real schools: they were not about experiences or consequences, learning or attitudes, but about creating tests that would be more accurate by following strict criteria. The tests discussed in graduate school belonged to the *big testing paradigm*, such as the TOEFL or the SAT, and not to tests given by teachers to students regularly in classes and schools as part of learning. The latter were simply viewed as irrelevant.

This was all in the era when language testing as an academic field had just begun to emerge. There were no *language* testing courses and only a very limited number of books on the topic. It was even before the journal *Language Testing* was born, about the time that the Canale and Swain model (1980) emerged and LTRC met for the first time.[†] One could find only occasional articles about language testing, mostly in journals such as *TESOL Quarterly* or the *Modern Language Journal*.

But it was also at this time that the FSI Oral Interview started spreading into academic communities, after being used exclusively by U.S. government agencies. It seemed like a very attractive test. It was the only test at the time in which people were asked to actually speak, to actually use language, in a face-to-face interaction. It was also attractive because the assessment of speaking was not based on scores and points of correct and incorrect words or phrases, but rather on a hierarchical scale that had broad definitions of language use.

My own research interest in those days, and for several years after, was directed at questions of test bias and method effects, addressing issues such as who was hurt and who benefited from certain language testing methods? How biased were certain testing methods? Should multiple choice or open-ended questions be used on language tests, and for whom? Should test questions be posed in L1 or L2? What other kinds of interactions could be used for testing oral proficiency to better reflect *real-life* oral interactions, in addition

---

[†][Ed. note: See Bachman, Chapter 3, for a discussion of early models of language proficiency and early meetings of LTRC.]

to the oral interview, which was the single dominating method for assessing speaking at the time? Were specific tests or testing methods marginalizing certain students? Who were the most accurate raters for oral tests? What topics were being covered on oral tests, and were they appropriate for all students, for all populations?

It was my involvement in introducing a new oral English test battery, using multiple and varied types of oral interactions, into the Israeli secondary school system as part of a high school graduation test battery in English as a foreign language (Shohamy, Bejarano, and Reves, 1986), that made me wear different glasses. It was then that I began to see that none of the psychometric qualities of tests I had learned about in graduate school really mattered to policy makers. When it came to the Ministry of Education, the policy decision to introduce the new oral tests was based on different sets of calculations. The introduction of oral tests was not about accuracy of the results but rather about gaining a tool that could influence and control the teaching of languages in the classrooms of the whole nation. It was then that I began to understand the crucial role that tests played as instruments in political, educational, and social contexts. It was then that I observed how tests served as policy tools to be used by educational systems primarily to promote a variety of agendas and to exercise power and control. Specifically, in the case of the oral test, and in many other examples, the main purpose was to enforce the teaching of oral language in the classroom and the utilization of specific methods, materials, and tasks. Tests, I realized, were tools in the hands of policy makers used to impose and perpetuate specific agendas. I have since researched and discussed these issues in numerous publications, and more extensively in the book *The Power of Tests* (2001). Along the way, I also realized how detached we language testers are from the political, social, and educational realities in which our language tests operate and how blind we often are to the political realities and contexts.

Since then I have become very aware of the strong influence of tests on educational systems, of their ability to dictate teaching and learning methods, to define language knowledge, to determine what is considered correct language and what is not, to determine language hierarchies, to determine language priorities such as which languages count in given contexts, to perpetuate monolingual realities and suppress multilingualism, and to continue to perpetuate the imagined criterion of *the native speaker*.

These realizations led me to pursue a somewhat different direction in language testing, that is, a focus on the use of language tests in political, social, and educational contexts. I now believe that there is a need to study issues of test use and consequences and to focus on the impact and ramifications of tests and the motivations for introducing them. We need to study how language tests affect people, societies, teachers, teaching, students, schools, language policies, and language itself. We need to examine the ramifications of tests, their uses, misuses, ethicality, power, biases, and the discrimination and language realities they create for certain groups and for nations, and we need to use a *critical language testing* perspective. All these topics fall under the theoretical legitimacy of Messick's (1994, 1996) work on the consequences and values of tests.

There are others in the field of language testing who ask similar questions: Lynch, Spolsky, Davies, Hamp-Lyons, McNamara, Norton, Elder, Cheng, Kunnan, Fulcher, to name just a few who examine different dimensions and perspectives on these issues. Because of this interest, language testing took a critical turn: it posed questions, it introduced doubts, it raised ethical issues, and it focused on fairness, responsibility, societies, and washback. It got us engaged in developing the ILTA (International Language Testing Association) *Code of Ethics* (2000) and discussing these issues at conferences on language testing and applied linguistics, in journal articles, and especially in the more recently founded journal, *Language Assessment Quarterly*.

Current Use of Tests in Education and Society

Yet, the current reality of tests, not only of *language* tests, is that they are given more power than ever, as they are widely used by governments, institutions, and central authorities world-wide. There is often a feeling that bureaucrats, educators, and political leaders have discovered an effective formula for providing the illusion that tests will solve all educational, political, and economic ills. Tests are currently used as the main instruments for educational reforms. Furthermore, in many countries language tests are used as gatekeepers to prevent the entry of unwanted people, such as immigrants and refugees, and thus to resolve national and international political issues. In the next part of this paper I will use a number of examples to show how tests are used for such purposes in education and society. I am at the same time claiming that it is also through the power of tests that progressive and open views can be negotiated and introduced.

Education

Education has always been a domain in which tests are used extensively for promoting and perpetuating multiple agendas. However, in the U.S., the No Child Left Behind (NCLB) Act (2002) provides a vivid illustration of how tests can be used aggressively and with only limited attempts to examine their consequences. The NCLB is anchored in law; it is sweeping in the sense that all students in U.S. public schools have to be tested, including recently arrived immigrants. Strong sanctions such as the closing of schools may be imposed on schools and teachers when students fail, and there are very limited possible repairs for schools whose students do not do well on these tests. Evans and Hornberger (2005) show how the NCLB perpetuates negative effects on bilingual education in the U.S. Byrnes (2005) in the *Modern Language Journal*'s "Perspectives," includes articles that specifically show how the NCLB decreases students' motivations to learn foreign languages and schools' motivations to teach them, as they are not included in the NCLB; rather, students and schools invest in learning and teaching English, the language that is being tested. Like many other national tests that are imposed by governments and ministries of education, the NCLB is a powerful educational tool that creates *de facto* language policies. It perpetuates national languages as the only alternative, since all NCLB tests are offered in the dominant and hegemonic language, English, thus sending an indirect message regarding the irrelevance of other languages, especially languages of immigrants and indigenous groups.

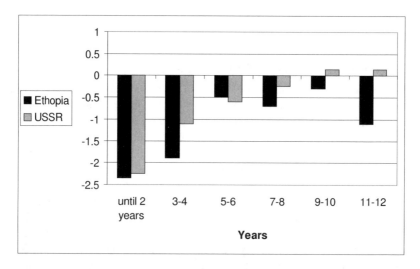

Figure 8.1: Ninth-grade Hebrew standard grades, according to years of residence

Further, while research has consistently shown that it takes a long time for immigrant students to reach equivalent levels of academic proficiency in the national language used for instruction in school, these tests expect immigrant students to reach levelss equivalent to those of students born into the language in an unrealistically short period of time, as they are tested through the medium of the new language a short time after immigration. Tests similar to those of the NCLB are administered in many nations nowadays. For example, Figures 8.1 and 8.2 are based on a national study conducted in Israel with Russian and Ethiopian immigrant students (Levin, Shohamy, and Spolsky, 2003). The graphs point to the length of time it takes immigrant students to acquire similar levels of academic achievement in Hebrew and mathematics in relation to students of the same age who were born in Israel. Figure 8.1 demonstrates that it takes Russian immigrant students 9–10 years to achieve scores similar to those of native speakers. Ethiopian immigrants never achieve similar levels of academic proficiency.

Figure 8.2 shows similar results in mathematics; the graph illustrates, again, that it takes the Russian immigrants about 9–10 years to obtain scores similar to those of native speakers.

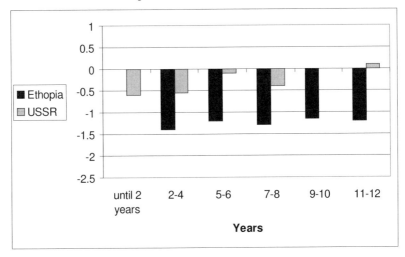

Figure 8.2: Eleventh-grade math standard grades, according to years of residence

The study measured these achievements in grades 5, 9, and 11. While slight variations occurred according to grade level, by and large the findings were the same showing consistently that immigrant students require 7, 9, or 11 years to attain equivalent levels of proficiency. It is especially revealing to focus on immigrant students from the former USSR, who generally arrive in Israel from educational contexts that provided them with high levels of mathematical knowledge and L1 literacy. Nevertheless, it takes them many years to reach levels of proficiency similar to those of the native speaker groups both in mathematics and language. The low achievement of the Ethiopian students is related to language mastery but may also involve other factors, as they do not come from an educational system that emphasizes advanced mathematics.

In spite of similar findings from other contexts (Thomas and Collier, 1997), indicating the length of time it takes immigrant students to acquire academic proficiency after they arrive, tests are often administered very soon after arrival, much before they are able to reach acceptable levels of proficiency, and poor results may lead to sanctions for students and for schools where the immigrants are enrolled. Clearly, administering these tests in an unfamiliar language negatively affects the performance of immigrant students and may classify them, inaccurately and unfairly, as having limited academic potential.

The important role that language plays in the academic success of students can be demonstrated via a number of different types of analyses. One such method is the comparison of performance of students on academic tests that are presented in different forms with different accommodations. Figure 8.3 shows the performance of immigrant students on the same math test presented in two different forms, one a bilingual form in Hebrew and Russian, and one, to an equivalent control group, in Hebrew only. The results presented in Figure 8.3 show the difference in performance when the Russian immigrants were accommodated using the bilingual mathematics test version in comparison to a group of Russian immigrant students who received no accommodation, the questions were presented in Hebrew only. As Figure 8.3 shows, the group that received the bilingual version of the math test performed significantly better than the monolingual group. Thus, the group presented with the test in a bilingual format enjoyed a significant academic advantage over the control group (Hebrew presentation only). These differences persisted for up to 8 years after immigration, indicating that immigrants continued to create and construct meaning through utilizing elements from their L1 for a long time after arrival in the new country.

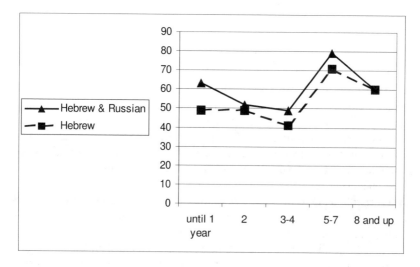

Figure 8.3: Math grades in monolingual vs. bilingual test versions

Given these results, one wonders what effect the presentation of tests with no such accommodations may have on the performance of immigrant students on tests such as those used in the NCLB program. In these tests immigrant students are expected to demonstrate their academic knowledge exclusively through the new language. This ignores the fact that learning to function in a new national language is a long and complicated process, whereby meaning is created and constructed via multiple channels (Bialystok, 2001; Abedi, 2004; Solano-Flores and Trumbell, 2003).

The use of tests in such ways leads to a number of questions such as: Should tests be used as tools for educational reform? Does the administration of national tests lead to improved education and improved achievement? Are these tests a true reflection of academic language? Who benefits from such tests and who pays the price? What are the results of tests being used for? What are the *real* agendas behind introducing national tests? Is the use of such tests an attempt to create and perpetuate policies that are detached from what is known about learning? Finally, and of crucial importance here, what should the role of language testers be in supporting or objecting to the use of tests for such policies?

Society

The other example that illustrates current uses of tests to exercise power and control is in the area of national policies. The main example used here is the current use of language tests in a growing number of countries as a condition for right of entry, residence, and citizenship.

Many countries, especially in Europe, including Britain, Latvia, and the Netherlands, as well as the U.S., are administering language citizenship tests, and a number of other countries, such as Australia, are seriously exploring this possibility. The idea behind such tests is the belief that language proficiency, as exemplified through these language tests, is an expression of loyalty and patriotism and should be a requirement for residency, and especially for citizenship. It should be noted that citizenship is generally required for obtaining benefits and access to social security, health, education, and election rights. In the Netherlands, for example, language tests in Dutch are administered to prospective immigrants even before their arrival in the Netherlands as a requirement for immigration, in the name of social cohesion. The term *naturalization* in the U.S. context is revealing in terms of the ideology behind citizenship and the connections seen between language, patriotism, and negative views of diversity. In an era of globalization, relatively free borders, and trans-nationalism, language tests become the major tools for imposing societal uniformity and a way to gatekeep those whom nations view as undesirable.

In this case language tests serve as tools through which those who are not proficient in the hegemonic language are de-legitimized and marginalized in the places where they reside, in the workplace as well as in higher education, thus contributing to the creation of second-class citizens and often leading to their expulsion. It is through language tests that such outcomes obtain legitimacy, as people are judged based on their language proficiency, and often at a level that is unrealistic for them to achieve.

Many questions arise with regard to the use of such citizenship tests: Why language? Why language tests? Why should language be considered a requirement of citizenship? How able are immigrants to acquire new languages at a certain stage of their lives or even to become successful in taking tests of a Western nature after being schooled elsewhere? Why is there a need to perpetuate national ideologies through language tests? (Are people possessions of states?) And why are language testers cooperating with policies that can lead to discrimination and gatekeeping?

Reactions and Actions

Given the above cases, and many others not discussed in this chapter, what is our role as language testers in being involved in supporting or rejecting such uses of tests given their potential consequences with regard to social justice? As is argued in Shohamy (2006), language tests are not neutral. Rather, they can determine language priorities and language hierarchies. They are capable of suppressing, eliminating, and marginalizing other languages; they can perpetuate national and hegemonic languages; they can define language knowledge and stipulate criteria for correctness (i.e., *the native variety*); and they can lead to the expulsion of people. Thus, as language testers we may at times find ourselves standing behind such acts and the use of language tests, uses, and consequences that may: lead to discrimination against those not proficient in the status languages, deny personal rights to those who cannot speak certain languages, marginalize other languages and other people who represent languages that are not tested, and perpetuate beliefs about language correctness, monolingualism, and the discrete boundaries of languages.

These are some of the questions and issues that need to be addressed by our profession: Are language tests always necessary? Do we, via our tests, contribute to an unequal world and harm social justice? Do our tests represent real language the way it is currently understood and used? Is the language we measure embedded in real and meaningful content? Do we provide legitimacy to discrimination, racism, xenophobia, and various political, social, economic, and personal agendas?

There is a need, I believe, for a deeper and more comprehensive understanding of language testing and its consequences, starting with those of us who work in this profession and then ensuring that educators, politicians, and others also gain such understanding. Given such an expanded understanding, we need to get engaged in a political debate about language awareness and language testing activism so we can influence those with better access to power centers, educational systems, law making, and especially the implementation of language-related policies.

But for that to happen, languages testers need also to adopt a more open view of what we assess, i.e., *language*. We need to ask ourselves what construct of language we are working with and whether through the use of monolingual language tests that have very clear and discrete boundaries we are contributing to an unrealistic view of language that is more of an imagined construct than a reality. Do we stand behind tests that lead to narrow and unrealistic criteria of correctness, limited views of grammaticality, perpetuating specific accents, re-enforcing the construct of the native speaker variety and contributing to the suppression of multilingualism in societies — attitudes that may be promoted by nation states? In the case of immigrants, for example, it is known that they continue to construct meaning by using both L1 and L2 for a long time after entering the school system, a finding supported by Figure 8.3 in this chapter. This reality, which is not yet recognized by educational systems, is denied by the continuing use of monolingual tests. Users of languages, especially in multilingual societies, the dominant pattern nowadays, create meanings via hybrids and fusions. Thus, language tests need to reflect such multilingual realities, where meanings are created through mixes, hybrids, and fusions, where different codes are used for the purpose of communication and expression and where languages do not have such distinct boundaries as linguists have led us to believe. Furthermore, multiple codes exist within every language: that is, languages are also known to consist of elements such as visuals, pictures, images, music, art, graphs, and a variety of symbols with varied ways of "languaging" (Shohamy, 2006) and cross-linguistic language boundaries (Kress and van Leeuwen, 1996; Kress, 2003, 2001). As language testers we need to ask ourselves whether our tests reflect such "languages" and whether by overlooking such realities we are contributing to an unrealistic view of language, counter to its natural use in communication, and perpetuating artificial standards of correctness, homogeneity, purity, and other imagined normative features. As language testers we need to think of tests that will accommodate a broader construct of what we mean by language today. We need to consider multi-coded language tests that will represent multilingual and multimodal realities; this is especially relevant when English, a global language that is deeply embedded in most other languages in education, commerce, and academic life, is involved (Canagarajah, 2006). At the same time we need to be more aware of the misuses of tests, demonstrate their effects and ramifications, and protect the victims of *bad testing* in ways that can lead to more inclusion, participation, and recognition that is not just channeled through majority languages.

Given the above discussion, as language testers we need to better understand the powerful role that language tests play in creating *de facto* language policies, often operating covertly and implicitly, yet with strong ramifications in terms of academic, personal, and human rights (Shohamy, 2006). Finally, regardless of the possible detrimental effects of tests in many domains, it is clear that tests are here to stay. That being the case, we need to begin exploring new ways through which these powerful and influential tools, given their consequences and ramifications, can be diverted towards creating positive, constructive, liberal, democratic, just, and negotiated tools that are capable of providing benefits, awards, privileges, language rights and freedom of speech. Tests need to be used not just to penalize *bad and impure languages* but to encourage the complex language varieties that are used among the diverse populations in this world and by extension to avoid the imposition of unrealistic criteria that serve only the privileged.

There is so much more to do; our work has only just begun ...

THE GOALS OF ILTA

1. Stimulate professional growth through workshops and conferences.
2. Promote the publication and dissemination of information related to the field of language testing.
3. Develop and provide for leadership in the field of language testing.
4. Provide professional services to its members.
5. Increase public understanding and support of language testing as a profession.
6. Build professional pride among its membership.
7. Recognize outstanding achievement among its membership.
8. Cooperate with other groups interested in language testing.
9. Cooperate with other groups interested in applied linguistics or measurement.

For more information regarding ILTA and how to become a member, please visit the ILTA website at www.iltaonline.com. ILTA is currently engaged in developing the Code of Practice (see the ILTA website for details). The members of ILTA meet annually at the Language Testing Research Colloquium (LTRC). See the reverse side of this page for a complete listing of all the LTRCs from 1979 to 2007.

LANGUAGE TESTING RESEARCH COLLOQUIA
1979 – 2007

1st	Boston, Massachusetts, United States	1979
2nd	San Francisco, California, United States	1980
3rd	Ann Arbor, Michigan, United States	1981
4th	Honolulu, Hawaii, United States	1982
5th	Ottawa, Ontario, Canada	1983
6th	Houston, Texas, United States	1984
7th	Princeton, New Jersey, United States	1985
8th	Monterey, California, United States	1986
9th	Miami Beach, Florida, United States	1987
10th	Urbana, Illinois, United States	1988
11th	San Antonio, Texas, United States	1989
12th	San Francisco, California, United States	1990
13th	Princeton, New Jersey, United States	1991
14th	Vancouver, British Columbia, Canada	1992
15th	Cambridge, United Kingdom, and Arnhem, The Netherlands	1993
16th	Washington, D.C., United States	1994
17th	Long Beach, California, United States	1995
18th	Tampere, Finland	1996
19th	Orlando, Florida, United States	1997
20th	Monterey, California, United States	1998
21st	Tsukuba, Japan	1999
22nd	Vancouver, British Columbia, Canada	2000
23rd	St. Louis, Missouri, United States	2001
24th	Hong Kong	2002
25th	Reading, United Kingdom	2003
26th	Temecula, California, United States	2004
27th	Ottawa, Ontario, Canada	2005
28th	Melbourne, Australia	2006
29th	Barcelona, Spain	2007

NOTES ON CONTRIBUTORS

J. Charles Alderson is Professor of Linguistics and English Language Education at the University of Lancaster. He was Scientific Coordinator of DIALANG 1999–2002 (www.dialang.org). He is internationally well known for his research and publications in language testing, including 17 books, 79 articles in refereed journals and chapters in books, 19 other publications, including research reports, 165 papers presented at professional conferences and seminars, and 197 seminars, workshops, and consultancies.

Lyle F. Bachman is Professor and Chair, Department of Applied Linguistics and TESL, University of California, Los Angeles. His current research interests include validation theory, assessing the academic achievement and English proficiency of English language learners in schools, assessing foreign language proficiency, interfaces between second language acquisition and language testing research, and epistemological issues in applied linguistics research. His most recent publication is *Statistical Analyses for Language Assessment* (Cambridge, 2004).

Andrew D. Cohen is Professor of Applied Linguistics, MA in ESL Program, University of Minnesota, Minneapolis. His research interests are in language learner strategies, pragmatics, language assessment, and research methods. Recent scholarly efforts include an ELT Advantage online course on assessing language ability in adults (Thomson Heinle) and *Language Learner Strategies: 30 Years of Research and Practice* (co-edited with Ernesto Macaro, OUP, September 2007).

Alan Davies is Emeritus Professor of Applied Linguistics in the University of Edinburgh. One-time editor of the journals *Applied Linguistics* and *Language Testing*, he was founding Director of the Language Testing Research Centre in the University of Melbourne. His research interests are in language assessment in relation to World Englishes and in the concept of the native speaker. Recent publications include *The Native Speaker: Myth and Reality* (Multilingual Matters, 2003) and *A Glossary of Applied Linguistics* (Lawrence Erlbaum, 2005).

Anne Lazaraton is an Associate Professor of English as a Second Language at the University of Minnesota where she teaches courses in ESL methodology, language analysis, practicum, discourse analysis, and language assessment. Her book, *A Qualitative Approach to the Validation of Oral Language Tests*, was published by Cambridge University Press in 2002. Her current research interests include teacher talk and presidential bullying of the press.

Tim McNamara is Professor of Applied Linguistics at The University of Melbourne in Australia. His research interests include language testing and language and identity. He is the author of *Language Testing* (OUP, 2000) and (with Carsten Roever) *Language Testing: The Social Dimension* (Blackwell, 2006).

Elana Shohamy is Professor of Language Education, School of Education, Tel-Aviv University. Her research focus on political and educational dimensions of language tests and topics related to language policy in multilingual societies. Her recent books are: *The Power of Tests: Critical Perspective of the Use of Language Tests* (Longman, 2001), and *Language Policy: Hidden Agendas and New Approaches* (Taylor & Francis Group, 2006). She is the current editor of the journal *Language Policy*.

Bernard Spolsky was born in New Zealand. He studied there and in Canada, and has taught in New Zealand, Australia, England, the United States and Israel. He retired as professor emeritus in 2000, and since then has continued writing and lecturing, mainly on language policy. His book *Language Policy* was published in 2004, and he is currently writing a book on language management and editing the Blackwell Handbook of Educational Linguistics. He received the ILTA–UCLES Award for Lifetime Achievement in Language Testing and has been elected an honorary member of the Japan Language Testing Association.

Lynda Taylor is Assistant Director of the Research and Validation Group within Cambridge ESOL, where she assists in coordinating the ESOL research program and disseminating research outcomes. She has extensive experience of theoretical and practical issues in language assessment. Current interests include the testing of speaking/writing, as well as the impact of linguistic variety on language assessment. Recent publications include an article in *ELT Journal* and a co-edited volume, *IELTS Collected Papers*.

REFERENCES

Abanomey, A. (2002). *The effect of texts' authenticity on reading-comprehension test-taking strategies used by adult Saudi learners of English as a foreign language.* PhD dissertation, Arizona State University.

Abedi, J. (2004). The No Child Left Behind Act and English language learners: Assessment and accountability issues. *Educational Researcher, 33*(1), 4–14.

ACTFL proficiency guidelines. (1983). Hastings-on-Hudson, NY: American Council on the Teaching of Foreign Languages.

ACTFL. (1985). *ACTFL Proficiency guidelines (revised).* Hastings-on-Hudson, NY: ACTFL Materials Center.

Alderson, J. C. (1981a). Reaction to the Morrow paper (3). In J. C. Alderson & A. Hughes (eds.), *Issues in language testing* (pp. 45–54). ELT documents 111. London: British Council.

Alderson, J. C. (1981b). Report of the discussion on communicative language testing. In J. C. Alderson & A. Hughes (eds.), *Issues in language testing* (pp. 55–65). ELT documents 111. London: British Council.

Alderson, J. C. (1983). Response to Harrison: Who needs jam? In A. Hughes & D. Porter (eds.), *Current developments in language testing* (pp. 87–92). London: Academic Press.

Alderson, J. C. (1991). Bands and scores. In J. C. Alderson & B. North (eds.), *Language testing in the 1990s: The communicative legacy* (pp. 71–86). London: Modern English Publications, in association with Macmillan.

Alderson, J. C. (1993). Judgments in language testing. In D. Douglas & C. Chapelle (eds.), *A new decade of language testing* (pp. 46–57). Arlington, VA: TESOL.

Alderson, J. C. (2005). *Diagnosing foreign language proficiency: The interface between learning and assessment.* London: Continuum.

Alderson, J. C., Figueras, N., Kuijper, H., Nold, G., Takala, S. & Tardieu, C. (2004). *The development of specifications for item development and classification within the Common European Framework of Reference for languages: Learning, teaching, assessment: Reading and listening. Final Report of the Dutch CEF Construct Project.* Lancaster: Lancaster University.

Alderson, J. C., Figueras, N., Nold, G., North, B., Takala, S. & Tardieu, C. (2006). Analysing tests of reading and listening in relation to the Common European Framework of Reference: The experience of the Dutch CEFR Construct Project. *Language Assessment Quarterly, 3*(1), 3–30.

Alderson, J. C. & Hughes, A. (eds.). (1981). *Issues in language testing.* London: British Council.

Allan, A. (1992). Development and validation of a scale to measure test-wiseness in EFL/ESL reading test-takers. *Language Testing, 9*(2), 101–122.

Anderson, M. L. (2003). Embodied cognition: A field guide. *Artificial Intelligence, 149*, 91–130.

Anderson, N. J. (1989). *Reading comprehension tests versus academic reading: What are second language readers doing?* PhD dissertation, University of Texas at Austin.

Anderson, N. J. (1991). Individual differences in strategy use in second language reading and testing. *The Modern Language Journal, 75*(4), 460–472.

Anderson, N. J., Bachman, L. F., Perkins, K. & Cohen, A. D. (1991). An exploratory study into the construct validity of a reading comprehension test: Triangulation of data sources. *Language Testing, 8*(1), 41–66.

Atkinson, J. M. & Heritage, J. (eds.). (1984). *Structures of social action: Studies in conversation analysis.* Cambridge: Cambridge University Press.

Bachman, L. F. (1990). *Fundamental considerations in language testing.* Oxford: Oxford University Press.

Bachman, L. F. (2000). Modern language testing at the turn of the century: Assuring that what we count counts. *Language Testing, 17*, 1–42.

Bachman, L. F. (2002). Some reflections on task-based language performance assessment. *Language Testing, 19*(4), 453–476.

Bachman, L. F. (May, 2004). Some current trends and issues in language assessment. Paper presented at the International Conference on Tertiary/College English Teaching, Nanjing, China.

Bachman, L. F. (2005). Building and supporting a case for test use. *Language Assessment Quarterly, 2*(1), 1–34.

Bachman, L. F. (2006). Generalizability: A journey into the nature of empirical research in applied linguistics. In M. Chalhoub-Deville, C. Chapelle & P. Duff (eds.), *Inference and generalizability in applied linguistics: Multiple perspectives* (pp. 165–207). Dordrecht: John Benjamins.

Bachman, L. F. & Cohen, A. D. (eds.) (1998). *Interfaces between second language acquisition and language testing research.* Cambridge: Cambridge University Press.

Bachman, L. F. & Palmer, A. (1980). The construct validation of oral proficiency tests. *TESL Studies, 3*, 1–20.

Bachman, L. F. & Palmer, A. (1981). The construct validation of the FSI oral interview. *Language Learning, 31*(1), 67–86.

Bachman, L. F. & Palmer, A. (1996). *Language testing in practice: Designing and developing useful language tests.* Oxford: Oxford University Press.

Bailey, A. L. & Butler, F. A. (2004). Ethical considerations in the assessment of the language and content knowledge of English language learners K–12. *Language Assessment Quarterly, 1*, 177–193.

Banerjee, J. & Franceschina, F. (February 2006). Documenting features of written language production typical at different IELTS band score levels. Paper presented at the ESF SCSS Exploratory Workshop "Bridging the gap between research on second language acquisition and research on language testing," Amsterdam, The Netherlands.

Banerjee, J. & Luoma, S. (1997). Qualitative approaches to test validation. In C. Clapham & D. Corson (eds.), *Encyclopedia of language and education*, Vol. 7: *Language testing and assessment* (pp. 275–287). Amsterdam: Kluwer.

Barnwell, D. (1996). *A history of foreign language testing in the United States: From its beginnings to the present.* Tempe, AZ: Bilingual Press.

Bennett, R. E. (1998). *Reinventing assessment: Speculations on the future of large-scale educational testing.* Princeton, NJ: Educational Testing Service.

Bialystok, E. (2001). *Bilingualism and development.* Cambridge: Cambridge University Press.

Brindley, G. (1994). Task-centred assessment in language learning: The promise and the challenge. In N. Bird, P. Falvey, A. B. M. Tsui, D. Allison & A. McNeill (eds.), *Language and learning* (pp. 73–94). Hong Kong: Institute of Language in Education, Hong Kong Department of Education.

Brindley, G. (1998). Outcomes-based assessment and reporting in language learning programmes: A review of the issues. *Language Testing, 15*(1), 45–85.

Brindley, G. (2001). Outcomes-based assessment in practice: Some examples and emerging insights. *Language Testing, 18*(4), 393–407.

Brindley, G. & Ross, S. (2001). EAP assessment: Issues, models and outcomes. In M. Peacock & J. Flowerdew (eds.), *English for academic purposes*, pp. 148–168. Cambridge: Cambridge University Press.

Brindley, G. & Slatyer, H. (2002). Exploring task difficulty in ESL listening assessment. *Language Testing, 19*(4), 369–394.

Broadfoot, P. (2005). Dark alleys and blind bends: Testing the language of learning. *Language Testing, 22*(2), 123–141.

Brown, A. (2003). Interviewer variation and the co-construction of speaking proficiency. *Language Testing 20*(1), 1–25.

Brown, A. (2005). *Interviewer variability in language proficiency interviews.* Frankfurt: Peter Lang.

Brown, A. & McNamara, T. (2004). 'The devil is in the detail': Researching gender issues in language assessment. *TESOL Quarterly 38*(3), 524–538.

Brown, J. D., Hudson, T., Norris, J. & Bonk, W. (2002). *An investigation of second language task-based performance assessments.* SLTCC Technical Report 24. Honolulu: Second Language Teaching & Curriculum Center, University of Hawai'i at Manoa.

Butler, J. (1990). *Gender trouble: Feminism and the subversion of identity.* New York: Routledge.

Butler, F. A., & Stevens, R. (2001). Standardised assessment of the content knowledge of English language learners K–12: Current trends and old dilemmas. *Language Testing, 18*(4), 409–427.

Byrnes, H. (2005). Perspectives. *Modern Language Journal, 89*(2), 248–282

Campbell, D. & Fiske, D. (1959). Convergent and discriminant validation by the multitrait–multimethod matrix. *Psychological Bulletin, 56*, 81–105.

Canagarajah, S. (2006). Changing communicative needs, revised assessment objectives: Testing English as an international language. *Language Assessment Quarterly, 3*(3), 229–242.

Canale, M. (1983). On some dimensions of language proficiency. In J. W. Oller, Jr. (ed.), *Issues in language testing research.* Rowley, MA: Newbury House.

Canale, M. & Swain, M. (1980). Theoretical bases of communicative approaches to second language teaching and testing. *Applied Linguistics, 1*(1), 1–47.

Candlin, C. (1987). Towards task-based learning. In C. Candlin & D. Murphy (eds.), *Language learning tasks*. Englewood Cliffs, NJ: Prentice-Hall.

Carroll, J. B. (1953). *Some principles of language testing: Report of the fourth annual roundtable meeting on languages and linguistics*. Washington, DC: Institute of Languages and Linguistics, Georgetown University.

Carroll, J. B. (1961). Fundamental considerations in testing for English proficiency of foreign students. In *Testing the English proficiency of foreign students* (pp. 30–40). Washington, DC: Center for Applied Linguistics.

Carroll, J. B. (1968). The psychology of language testing. In A. Davies (ed.), *Language testing symposium: A psycholinguistic approach* (pp. 46–69). London: Oxford University Press.

Carroll, J. B. (1973). Foreign language testing: Will the persistent problems persist? In M. O'Brien (ed.), *Testing in second language teaching: New dimensions* (pp. 6–17). Dublin: ATESOL-Ireland.

Carroll, J. B. (1980). *Testing communicative performance*. London: Pergamon.

Carroll, J. B. (1983). Psychometric theory and language testing. In J. W. Oller, Jr. (ed.), *Issues in language testing research* (pp. 80–105). Rowley, MA: Newbury House.

Carroll, J. B. (1986). LT+25, and beyond. *Language Testing, 3*(2), 123–129.

Carroll, J. B., Carton, A. S. & Wilds, C. (1959). *An investigation of "cloze" items in the measurement of achievement in foreign languages*. Cambridge, MA: Laboratory for Research in Instruction, Graduate School of Education, Harvard University.

Center for Applied Linguistics. (1961). *Testing the English proficiency of foreign students. Report of a conference sponsored by the Center for Applied Linguistics in cooperation with the Institute of International Education and the National Association of Foreign Student Advisers*. Washington, DC: Center for Applied Linguistics.

Chalhoub-Deville, M. (1995). A contextualized approach to describing oral language proficiency. *Language Learning, 45*(2), 251–281.

Chalhoub-Deville, M. (2003). Second language interaction: Current perspectives and future trends. *Language Testing, 20*(4), 369–383.

Chalhoub-Deville, M. & Deville, C. (2005). A look back at and forward to what language testers measure. In E. Hinkel (ed.), *Handbook of research in second language teaching and learning* (pp. 815–831). Mahwah, NJ: Lawrence Earlbaum.

Chalhoub-Deville, M. & Tarone, E. (1996). What is the role of specific contexts in second language acquisition, teaching and testing? Center for Advanced Research on Language Acquisition, University of Minnesota.

Chamot, A. & O'Malley, J. (1994). *The CALLA handbook: Implementing the cognitive academic language learning approach*. Reading, MA: Addison-Wesley.

Chapelle, C. (1994). Are C-tests valid measures for L2 vocabulary research? *Second Language Research, 10*, 157–187.

Chapelle, C. (1998). Construct definition and validity inquiry in SLA research. In L. F. Bachman & A. D. Cohen (eds.), *Interfaces between second language acquisition and language testing research* (pp. 32–70). New York: Cambridge University Press.

Cheng, L., Rogers, W. T. & Hu, H. (2004). ESL/EFL instructors' classroom assessment practices: Purposes, methods, and procedures. *Language Testing, 21*(3), 360–389.

Chomsky, N. (1957). *Syntactic structures.* Gravenhage: Mouton.

Chomsky, N. (1965). *Aspects of the theory of syntax.* Cambridge, MA: MIT Press.

Clapham, C. (1996). *The development of IELTS: A study of the effect of background knowledge on reading comprehension, Studies in Language Testing, 4.* Cambridge: UCLES/Cambridge University Press.

Clark, J. L. D. (1972). *Foreign language testing: Theory and practice.* Philadelphia: Center for Curriculum Development.

Clark, J. L. D. (1975). Theoretical and technical considerations in oral proficiency testing. In R. Jones & B. Spolsky (eds.), *Testing language proficiency* (pp. 10–24). Arlington, VA: Center for Applied Linguistics.

Clark, J. L. D. (1979). Direct vs. semi-direct tests of speaking ability. In E. Brière & F. Hinofotis (eds.), *Concepts in language testing: Some recent studies.* Washington, DC: TESOL.

Clay, M. M. (1979). *The early detection of reading difficulties: A diagnostic survey with recovery procedures.* Auckland, NZ: Heinemann.

Cohen, A. D. (1980). *Testing language ability in the classroom.* Rowley, MA: Newbury House.

Cohen, A. D. (1984). On taking language tests: What the students report. *Language Testing, 1*(1), 70–81.

Cohen, A. D. (2000). Exploring strategies in test-taking: Fine-tuning verbal reports from respondents. In G. Ekbatani & H. Pierson (eds.), *Learner-directed assessment in ESL* (pp. 127–150). Mahwah, NJ: Lawrence Erlbaum.

Cohen, A. D. (In press). Coming to terms with language learner strategies: Surveying the experts. In A. D. Cohen & E. Macaro (eds.), *Language learner strategies: 30 years of research and practice.* Oxford: Oxford University Press.

Cohen, A. D. & Aphek, E. (1979). *Easifying second language learning.* A research report under the auspices of Brandeis University and submitted to the Jacob Hiatt Institute, Jerusalem. Educational Resources Information Center, ED 163 753, 47 pp.

Cohen, A. D. & Brooks-Carson, A. (2001). Research on direct vs. translated writing: Students' strategies and their results. *Modern Language Journal, 85*(2), 169–188.

Cohen, A. D. & Macaro, E. (eds.) (In press). *Language learner strategies: 30 years of research and practice.* Oxford: Oxford University Press.

Cohen, A. D., Segal, M. & Weiss Bar-Siman-Tov, R. (1985). The C-test in Hebrew In C. Klein-Braley & U. Raatz (eds.), *C-Tests in der Praxis* (pp. 121–127). AKS Rundbrief Special Issue *13/14.* Bochum, Germany: Ruhr-Universität Bochum.

Cohen, A. D. & Upton, T. A. (2006). *Strategies in responding to the new TOEFL reading tasks.* Monograph No. 33. Princeton, NJ: Educational Testing Service. Retrieved October 20, 2006:
www.ets.org/Media/Research/pdf/RR-06-06.pdf.

Cooper, R. L. (1968). An elaborated language testing model. *Language Learning* (Special issue No. 7), 57–72.

Council of Europe. (2001). *A Common European Framework of Reference for Languages: Learning, teaching and assessment.* Cambridge: Cambridge University Press.

Coxhead, A. (1998). *An academic word list.* English Language Institute Occasional Publication, No. 18. Wellington: School of Linguistics and Applied Language Studies, Victoria University of Wellington.

Crookes, G. & Gass, S. (1993a). *Tasks and language learning: Integrating theory and practice.* Clevedon: Multilingual Matters.

Crookes, G. & Gass, S. (1993b). *Tasks in a pedagogical context: Integrating theory and practice.* Clevedon: Multilingual Matters.

Cunningham, J. & Moore, D. (1993). The contribution of understanding academic vocabulary to answering comprension questions. *Journal of Reading Behaviors, 25,* 171–180.

Darnell, D. K. (1968). *The development of an English language proficiency test of foreign students, using a clozentropy procedure* (Final report, Project #7-8-010, Grant OEG-8-070010-200(057)).

Darnell, D. K. (1970). Clozentropy: A procedure for testing English language proficiency of foreign students. *Speech monographs, 37,* 36–46.

Davidson, F. & Cho, Y. (2001). Issues in EAP Test Development: What one institutions and its history tell us. In M. Peacock & J. Flowerdew (eds.), *English for academic purposes,* pp. 286–297. Cambridge: Cambridge University Press.

Davies, A. (1965). *Proficiency in English as a second language.* PhD dissertation, University of Birmingham.

Davies, A. (1977). The construction of language tests. In J. P. B. Allen & A. Davies (eds.), *Testing and experimental methods* (pp. 38–104). London: Oxford University Press.

Davies, A. (1991). *The native speaker in applied linguistics.* Edinburgh: Edinburgh University Press.

Davies. A. (2007). *Assessing academic English: Testing English proficiency 1950–2005: The IELTS solution, Studies in Language Testing, 23.* Cambridge: UCLES/ Cambridge University Press.

Davies, A. (ed.). (1968). *Language testing symposium: a psycholinguistic perspective.* Oxford: Oxford University Press.

Dollerup, C, Glahn, E. & Rosenberg Hansen, C. (1982). Reading strategies and test-solving techniques in an EFL-reading comprehension test: A preliminary report. *Journal of Applied Language Study, 1*(1), 93–99.

Douglas, D. (1978). Simplified clozentropy: An analysis of L1 and L2 responses to reading texts. In V. Kohonen & N. E. Enkvist (eds.), *Text linguistics, cognitive learning and language teaching* (pp. 223–238). Turku: Finnish Association of Applied Linguistics.

Douglas, D. (2000). *Assessing language for specific purposes: Theory and practice.* Cambridge: Cambridge University Press.

Douglas, D. & Hegelheimer, V. (2005). Cognitive processes and use of knowledge in performing new TOEFL listening tasks. 2nd Interim Report to Educational Testing Service. Ames: Iowa State University.

Eades, D. (2005). Applied linguistics and language analysis in asylum seeker cases. *Applied Linguistics, 26*(4), 503–526.

Eades, D., Fraser, H., Siegel, J., McNamara, T. & Baker, B. (2003). Linguistic identification in the determination of nationality: A preliminary report. *Language Policy, 2*(2), 179–199.

Earl, L. (2003). *Assessment as learning*. Thousand Oaks, CA: Corwin Press.

Edelenbos, P. & Kubanek-German, A. (2004). Teacher assessment: The concept of 'diagnostic competence'. *Language Testing, 21*(3), 259–283.

Edgeworth, F. Y. (1888). The statistics of examinations. *Journal of the Royal Statistical Society, 51*, 599–635.

Edgeworth, F. Y. (1890). The element of chance in competitive examinations. *Journal of the Royal Statistical Society, 53*, 644–663.

Educational Testing Service. (1982). *ETS oral proficiency manual*. Princeton, New Jersey: Educational Testing Service.

Educational Testing Service. (1995). *TOEFL test preparation kit*. Princeton, NJ: Educational Testing Service.

Educational Testing Service. (2002). *LanguEdge Courseware: Handbook for scoring speaking and writing*. Princeton, NJ: Educational Testing Service.

Elder, C., Iwashita, N. & McNamara, T. (2002). Estimating the difficulty of oral proficiency tasks: What does the test-taker have to offer? *Language Testing, 19*(4), 347–368.

English Language Testing Service (ELTS). (1980). London: British Council.

English Proficiency Test Battery (EPTB). (1964). Short version form A, parts 1 and 2. London: British Council.

Enright, M. K., Grabe, W., Koda, K., Mosenthal, P., Mulcahy-Ernt, P., & Schedl, M. (2000). *TOEFL 2000: Reading Framework: A working paper*. Princeton: Educational Testing Service.

Evans, B. & Hornberger, N. (2005). Child left behind: Repealing and unpeeling federal language education policy in the United States. *Language Policy, 4*(1), 67–85.

Falvey, P. & Shaw, S. (2006). IELTS Writing: Revising assessment criteria and scales (Phase 5). *Research Notes, 23* (February), pp. 8–13, University of Cambridge ESOL Examinations.

Farhady, H. (1983). On the plausibility of the unitary language proficiency factor. In J. W. Oller, Jr. (ed.), *Issues in language testing research* (pp. 11–28). Rowley, MA: Newbury House.

Finoccchiaro, M. & Sako, S. (1983). *Foreign language testing: A practical approach*. New York: Regents.

Fishman, J. A. (1972). *The sociology of language*. Rowley, MA: Newbury.

Fishman, J. A., Cooper, R. L. & Ma, R. (1971). *Bilingualism in the barrio*. Bloomington, IN: Research Center for the Language Sciences, Indiana University.

Flowerdew, J. (1993). Concordancing as a tool in course design. *System, 21*, 231–244.

Forster, D. E. & Karn, R. (1998). *Teaching TOEIC/TOEFL test-taking strategies*. Paper presented at the 32nd Annual Conference of Teachers of English to Speakers of Other Languages, Seattle, WA, March 17–21, 1998. (ERIC Document Reproduction Service No. ED427543)

Foucault, M. (1972 [1969]). *The archaeology of knowledge*, trans. A. M. S. Smith. London: Routledge. [Originally published as *L'archeologie du savoir*. Paris: Gallimard (1969).]

Foucault, M. (1977 [1975]). *Discipline and punish: The birth of the prison*, trans. A. Sheridan. London: Allen Lane. [Originally published as *Surveiller et punir: Naissance de la prison*. Paris: Éditions Gallimard (1975).]

Franceschina, F. (2006). Introducing LANCAWE (Lancaster Corpus of Academic Written English). Paper presented at the Learner Corpus Colloquium, Learner Corpus Research Easter School, April 3, 2006. Centre for English Corpus Linguistics, University of Louvain, Louvain-la-Neuve, Belgium.

Fulcher, G. (1996). Does thick description lead to smart tests? A data-based approach to rating scale construction. *Language Testing, 13*(2), 208–238.

Fulcher, G. (2004a). Are Europe's tests being built on an 'unsafe' framework. *Education Guardian*, March 18.

Fulcher, G. (2004b). Deluded by artifices? The Common European Framework and harmonization. *Language Assessment Quarterly 1*(4), 253–266.

Gaies, S., Gradman, H. & Spolsky, B. (1977). Towards the measurement of functional proficiency: Contextualization of the noise test. *TESOL Quarterly, 11*, 51–57.

Gibbons, P. (1998). Classroom talk and the learning of new registers in a second language. *Language and Education, 12*, 99–118.

Gordon, C. (1987). The effect of testing method on achievement in reading comprehension tests in English as a foreign language. MA thesis, School of Education, Tel Aviv University.

Graduateshotline. (2006). *TOEFL*. Retrieved January 29, 2007: www.graduateshotline.com/toefl.html.

Green, A. (1998). *Verbal protocol analysis in language testing research: A handbook, Studies in Language Testing, 5*. Cambridge: UCLES/Cambridge University Press.

Grotjahn, R. (1986). Test validation and cognitive psychology: Some methodological considerations. *Language Testing, 3*(2), 159–185.

Grotjahn, R. (1987). How to construct and evaluate a C-Test: A discussion of some problems and some statistical analyses. In R. Grotjahn, C. Klein-Braley, & D. K. Stevenson (eds.), *Taking their measure: The validity and validation of language tests* (pp. 219–254). Bochum, Germany: Brockmeyer.

Hamp-Lyons, L. & Kroll, B. (1997). *TOEFL 2000: Writing, composition, community and assessment*. Princeton: Educational Testing Service.

Hamp-Lyons, L. (ed.). (1991). *Assessing second language writing in academic contexts*. Norwood, NJ: Ablex.

Harris, D. (1969). *Testing English as a second language*. New York: McGraw-Hill.

Harrison, A. (1983). Communicative testing: Jam tomorrow? In A. Hughes & D. Porter (eds.), *Current developments in language testing* (pp. 77–86). London: Academic Press.

Hartog, P. & Rhodes, E. C. (1935). *An Examination of examinations, being a summary of investigations on comparison of marks allotted to examination scripts by independent examiners and boards of examiners, together with a section on viva voce examinations*. London: Macmillan.

Hartog, P. & Rhodes, E. C. (1936). *The marks of examiners, being a comparison of marks allotted to examination scripts by independent examiners and boards of examiners, together with a section on viva voce examinations.* London: Macmillan and Company Ltd.

Hawkey, R. (2006). *Impact Theory and practice: Studies of IELTS and Progetto Lingue 2000, Studies in Language Testing, 24.* Cambridge: UCLES/Cambridge University Press.

He, A. & Young, R. (1998). Language proficiency interviews: A discourse approach. In R. Young & A. He (eds.), *Talking and testing* (pp. 1–24). Amsterdam: John Benjamins.

Heaton, J. (1975). *Writing English language tests.* London: Longman.

Heaton, J. (1988). *Writing English language tests.* 2nd ed. London: Longman.

Hill, A. A. (ed.). (1953). *Report of the fourth annual round table meeting on linguistics and language teaching.* Washington, DC: Georgetown University Press.

Hofer, B. & Pintrich, P. (1997). The development of epistemological theories: Beliefs about knowledge and knowing and their relation to learning. *Review of Educational Research, 67*(1), 88–140.

Holtzman, P. (1967). English language proficiency testing and the individual. In D. Wigglesworth (ed.), *ATESL Conference Papers* (pp. 76–84). Los Altos, CA: Language Research Associates Press.

Homburg, T. J. & Spaan, M. C. (1981). ESL Reading proficiency assessment: Testing strategies. In M. Hines & W. Rutherford (eds.), *On TESOL '81* (pp. 25–33). Washington, DC: TESOL.

Hughes, A. & Porter, D. (eds.). (1983). *Current developments in language testing.* London: Academic Press.

Huhta, A., Luoma, S., Oscarson, M., Sajavaara, K., Takala, S. & Teasdale, A. (2002). DIALANG: A diagnostic language assessment system for adult learners. In J. C. Alderson (ed.), *Common European Framework of Reference for languages: Learning, teaching, assessment. Case studies* (pp. 130–145). Strasbourg: Council of Europe.

Hyland, K. (2004). Patterns of engagement: Dialogic features and L2 undergraduate writing. In L. J. Ravelli & R. A. Ellis (eds.), *Analysing academic writing* (pp. 5–23). London: Continuum.

International English Language Testing System (IELTS). (1989; revised 1995). Cambridge: UCLES; London: British Council; Canberra: IDP.

ILTA Code of Ethics for Foreign/Second Language Testing. (2000). Vancouver, B.C.: International Language Testing Association.

Irvine, P., Atai, P. & Oller, J.W., Jr. (1974). Cloze, dictation and the test of English as a foreign language. *Language Learning, 24,* 245–252.

Jacoby, S. & McNamara, T. (1999). Locating competence. *English for Specific Purposes, 18*(3), 213–241.

Jacoby, S. & Ochs, E. (1995). Co-construction: An introduction. *Research on Language and Social Interaction, 28,* 171–183.

Jamieson, J., Jones, S., Kirsch, I., Mosenthal, P. & Taylor, C. (2000). *TOEFL 2000 framework: A working paper*. TOEFL Monograph Series MS-16. Princeton, NJ: Educational Testing Service.

Jones, R. (1979a). Performance testing of second language proficiency. In E. Brière & F. Hinofotis (eds.), *Concepts in language testing: Some recent studies* (pp. 50–57). Washington, DC: TESOL.

Jones, R. (1979b). The oral interview of the Foreign Service Institute. In B. Spolsky (ed.), *Some major tests* (pp. 104–115). Washington, DC: Center for Applied Linguistics.

Jones, R. (1985a). Second language performance testing: An overview. In P. Hauptman, R. LeBlanc & M. Wesche (eds.), *Second language performance testing* (pp. 15–24). Ottawa: University of Ottawa Press.

Jones, R. (1985b). Some basic considerations in testing oral proficiency. In Y. Lee, A. Fok, R. Lord & G. Low (eds.), *New directions in language testing* (pp. 77–84). Oxford: Pergamon.

Kaftandjieva, F. & Takala, S. (2006). *The mapping sentence guide to the galaxy of 'can dos'*. Retrieved June 29, 2006:
www.ealta.eu.org/conference/2006/docs/ Kaftandjieva&Takala_ealta2006.ppt

Kane, M. T. (1992). An argument-based approach to validation. *Psychological Bulletin, 112*, 527–553.

Klein-Braley, C. (1985). A close-up on the C test: A study in the construct validation of authentic tests. *Language Testing, 2*(1), 76–104.

Klein-Braley, C. (1997). C-tests in the context of reduced redundancy testing: An appraisal. *Language Testing, 14*(1), 47–84.

Klein-Braley, C. & Raatz, U. (1984). A survey of research on the C-Test. *Language Testing, 1*(2), 134–146.

König, K. & Perchinig, B. (2005). Austria. In J. Niessen, Y. Schibel & C. Thompson (eds.), *Current immigration debates in Europe: A publication of the European Migration Dialogue*. Retrieved January 11, 2007:
www.migpolgroup.com/documents/3055.html.

Kramsch, C. (1986). From language proficiency to interactional competence. *Modern Language Journal, 70*(4), 366–372.

Kress, G. (2003). *Literacy in the new media age*. London: Routledge.

Kress, G. & van Leeuwen, T. (1996) *Reading images: The grammar of visual design*. London: Routledge.

Kunnan, A. J. (2005a). 40 years in applied linguistics: An interview with Alan Davies. *Language Assessment Quarterly, 2*(1), 35–50.

Kunnan, A. J. (2005b). Language assessment from a wider context. In E. Hinkel (ed.), *Handbook of research on second language teaching and learning* (pp. 779–794). Mahwah, NJ: Lawrence Erlbaum.

Labov, W. (1972). *Sociolinguistic patterns*. Oxford: Blackwell.

Lado, R. (1961). *Language testing: The construction and use of foreign language tests*. London: Longman.

Language and National Origin Group. (2004). Guidelines for the use of language analysis in relation to questions of national origin in refugee cases. *The International Journal of Speech, Language and the Law, 11*(2), 261–266.

Latham, H. (1877). *On the action of examinations considered as a means of selection.* Cambridge: Deighton, Bell and Company.

Lazaraton, A. (2002). *A qualitative approach to the validation of oral language tests, Studies in Language Testing, 14.* Cambridge: UCLES/Cambridge University Press.

Lazaraton, A. (2003). Evaluative criteria for qualitative research in applied linguistics: Whose criteria and whose research? *Modern Language Journal, 87*, 1–12.

Lazaraton, A. (2004). Qualitative research methods in language test development and validation. In M. Milanovic & C. Weir (eds.), *European language testing in a global context: Proceedings of the ALTE Barcelona Conference, July 2001, Studies in Language Testing, 18* (pp. 51–71). Cambridge: UCLES/Cambridge University Press.

Lazaraton, A. & Frantz, R. (1997). An analysis of the relationship between task features and candidate output for the Revised FCE Speaking Test. Unpublished report for Cambridge ESOL.

Leung, C. & Mohan, B. (2004). Teacher formative assessment and talk in classroom contexts: Assessment as discourse and assessment of discourse. *Language Testing, 21*(3), 335–359.

Levin, T., Shohamy, E., & Spolsky, B. (2003). Academic achievements of immigrants in schools. Report submitted to the Ministry of Education. Tel Aviv University [in Hebrew].

Long, M. (1985). A role for instruction in second language acquisition: Task-based language teaching. In K. Hyltenstam & M. Pienemann (eds.), *Modelling and assessing second language acquisition* (pp. 77–99). Clevedon: Multilingual Matters.

Long, M. & Crookes, G. (1992). Three approaches to task-based syllabus design. *TESOL Quarterly, 26*(1), 27–56.

Lowry, D. T. & Marr, T. J. (1975). Clozentropy as a Measure of International Communication Comprehension. *Public Opinion Quarterly, 39*, 301.

Lumley, T. & Brown, A. (2004a). Test-taker and rater perspectives on integrated reading and writing tasks in the Next Generation TOEFL. *Language Testing Update, 35*, 75–79.

Lumley, T. & Brown, A. (2004b). *Test taker response to integrated reading/writing tasks in TOEFL: Evidence from writers, texts, and raters.* Final Report to ETS. Language Testing Research Centre, University of Melbourne.

Lumley, T. & Brown, A. (2005). Research methods in language testing. In E. Hinkel (ed.), *Handbook of research in second language teaching and learning* (pp. 833–855). Mahwah, NJ: Lawrence Erlbaum.

Madsen, H. (1983). *Techniques in testing.* Oxford: Oxford University Press.

McNamara, T. (1995). Modelling performance: Opening Pandora's box. *Applied Linguistics, 16*(2), 159–175.

McNamara, T. (1996). *Measuring second language performance.* London: Longman.

McNamara, T. (2001). Language assessment as social practice: Challenges for research. *Language Testing, 18*(4), 333–349.

McNamara, T., Hill, K. & May, L. (2002). Discourse and assessment. *Annual Review of Applied Linguistics, 22,* 221–242.

McNamara, T. & Lumley, T. (1997). The effect of interlocutor and assessment mode variables in overseas assessments of speaking skills in occupational settings. *Language Testing, 14*(2), 140–156.

McNamara, T. & Roever, C. (2006). *Language testing: The social dimension.* Oxford: Blackwell.

Macaulay, T. B. (1853). *Speeches, parliamentary and miscellaneous.* London: Henry Vizetelly.

Madaus, G. F. & Kellaghan, T. (1991). *Student examination systems in the European community: Lessons for the United States* (Contractor Report submitted to the Office of Technology Assessment, United States Congress).

Marinelli, V. (2005). The Netherlands. In J. Niessen, Y. Schibel & C. Thompson (eds.), *Current immigration debates in Europe: A publication of the European Migration Dialogue.* Retrieved January 11, 2007:
www.migpolgroup.com/documents/3055.html.

Messick, S. (1989). Validity. In R. L. Linn (ed.), *Educational measurement* (pp. 13–103). 3rd ed. New York: American Council on Education and Macmillan Publishing.

Messick, S. (1994). The interplay of evidence and consequences in the validation of performance assessment. *Educational Researcher, 23,* 13–23.

Messick, S. (1996). Validity and washback in language testing. *Language Testing, 13*(4), 241–257.

Milanovic, M. & Saville, N. (1994). An investigation of marking strategies using verbal protocols. Paper presented at 16th Language Testing Research Colloquium, March 1994, in Washington, DC.

Milanovic, M. & Saville, N. (1996). Introduction. In M. Milanovic & N. Saville (eds.), *Performance, testing, cognition and assessment: Selected papers from the 15th Language Testing Research Colloquium, Cambridge and Arnhem, Studies in Language Testing, 3* (pp. 92–114). Cambridge: UCLES/Cambridge University Press.

Milanovic, M., Saville, N. & Shuhong, S. (1996). A study of the decision-making behaviour of composition markers. In M. Milanovic & N. Saville (eds.), *Performance, testing, cognition and assessment: Selected papers from the 15th Language Testing Research Colloquium, Studies in Language Testing, 3* (pp. 1–17). Cambridge: UCLES/Cambridge University Press.

Monroe, P. (ed.). (1939). *Conference on examinations under the auspices of the Carnegie Corporation, the Carnegie Foundation, the International Institute of Teachers College, Columbia University, at the Hotel Royal, Dinard, France, September 16th to 19th, 1938.* New York City: Teachers College, Columbia University.

Morrow, K. (1979). Communicative language testing: revolution or evolution? In C. J. Brumfit & K. Johnson (eds.), *The communicative approach to language teaching* (pp. 143–157). Oxford: Oxford University Press.

Morrow, K. (1981). Communicative language testing: Revolution or evolution? In J. C. Alderson & A. Hughes (eds.), *Issues in language testing* (pp. 9–25). London: British Council.

Nation, P. (1990). *Teaching and learning vocabulary.* New York: Heinle & Heinle.

Nevo, N. (1989). Test-taking strategies on a multiple-choice test of reading comprehension. *Language Testing, 6*(2), 199–215.

No Child Left Behind Act. (2001). Public Law 107-110 (January 8, 2002). United States Congress.

Norris, J., Brown, J. D., Hudson, T. & Yoshioka, J. (1998). *Designing second language performance assessments. SLTCC Technical Report 18.* Honolulu: Second Language Teaching & Curriculum Center, University of Hawai'i at Manoa.

Nyhus, S. E. (1994). Attitudes of non-native speakers of English toward the use of verbal report to elicit their reading comprehension strategies. Plan B masters paper, Department of English as a Second Language, University of Minnesota, Minneapolis.

Oller, J. W., Jr. (1972). Scoring methods and difficulty levels for cloze tests of proficiency in English as a second language. *Modern Language Journal, 56,* 151–158.

Oller, J. W., Jr. (1975). *Research with cloze procedures in measuring the proficiency of non-native speakers of English: An annotated bibliography.* Washington DC: ERIC Clearinghouse on Language and Linguistics.

Oller, J. W., Jr. (1976). Evidence of a general language proficiency factor: An expectancy grammar. *Die neuren sprachen, 76,* 165–174.

Oller, J. W., Jr. (1979). *Language tests at school.* London: Longman.

Oller, J. W., Jr. (1983). A consensus for the eighties? In J. W. Oller, Jr. (ed.), *Issues in language testing research* (pp. 351–356). Rowley, MA: Newbury House.

Oller, J. W., Jr. & Hinofotis, F. (1980). Two mutually exclusive hypotheses about second language ability: Indivisible or partially divisible competence? In J. W. Oller, Jr. & K. Perkins (eds.), *Research in language testing* (pp. 13–23). Rowley, MA: Newbury House.

O'Malley, J. M. & Chamot, A. U. (1990). *Learning strategies in second language acquisition.* Cambridge: Cambridge University Press.

Oxford, R. L. (1990). *Language learning strategies: What every teacher should know.* New York: Newbury House/Harper & Row.

Palmer, A., Groot, P. & Trosper, G. (eds.). (1981). *The construct validation of tests of communicative competence.* Washington, DC: TESOL.

Pennycook, A. (1994). Incommensurable discourses? *Applied Linguistics, 15*(2), 115–138.

Phakiti, A. (2003). A closer look at the relationship of cognitive and metacognitive strategy use to EFL reading achievement test performance. *Language Testing, 20*(1), 26–56.

Pomerantz, A. & Fehr, B. J. (1997). Conversation analysis: An approach to the study of social action as sense making practices. In T. A. van dijk (ed.), *Discourse as social action, discourse studies: A multidisciplinary introduction* (pp. 64–91). London: Sage.

Pope, A. (1711). *An essay on criticism.* London: Lewis.

Psychological Corporation. (1997). *Language Aptitude Battery for the Japanese.* San Antonio, TX: Psychological Corporation.

Purpura, J. E. (1997). An analysis of the relationships between test-takers' cognitive and metacognitive strategy use and second language test performance. *Language Learning, 47*(2), 289–325.

Purpura, J. E. (1998). Investigating the effects of strategy use and second language test performance with high- and low-ability test-takers: A structural equation modelling approach. *Language Testing, 15*(3), 333–379.

Purpura, J. E. (1999). *Learner strategy use and performance on language tests: A structural equation modeling approach, Studies in Language Testing, 8*. Cambridge: UCLES/Cambridge University Press.

QSR International (2005). *NVivo 6* [software program]. http://www.qsrinternational.com.

Raatz, U. & Klein-Braley, C. (1981). The C-test: A modification of the cloze procedure. In T. Culhane, C. Klein-Braley, & D. K. Stevenson (eds.), *Practice and problems in language testing* (pp. 113–138). *University of Essex Occasional Papers 4*. Colchester: Department of Language and Linguistics, University of Essex.

Ravelli, L. J. & Ellis, R. A. (eds.). (2004). *Analysing academic writing*. London: Continuum.

Rea-Dickins, P. (2001). Mirror, mirror on the wall: Identifying processes of classroom assessment. *Language Testing, 18*(4), 429–462.

Read, J. (2000). *Assessing vocabulary*. Cambridge: Cambridge University Press.

Read, J. & Chapelle, C. (2001). A framework for second language assessment. *Language Testing, 18*(1), 1–32.

Reath, A. (2004). Language analysis in the context of the asylum process: Procedures, validity, and consequences. *Language Assessment Quarterly, 1*(4), 209–233.

Resnick, L. (ed.). (1993). *Cognition and instruction, 10*(2/3).

Richards, K. (2003). *Qualitative inquiry in TESOL*. Hampshire, UK: Palgrave Macmillan.

Rivera, C. (ed.). (1983). *An ethnographic/sociolinguistic approach to language proficiency assessment*. Clevedon: Multilingual Matters.

Rivera, C. (ed.). (1984). *Communicative competence approaches to language proficiency assessment: Research and application*. Clevedon: Multilingual Matters.

Roach, J. O. (1945). *Some problems of oral examinations in modern languages: An experimental approach based on the Cambridge Examinations in English for foreign students, being a report circulated to oral examiners and local examiners for those examinations*. Cambridge: Local Examinations Syndicate.

Rogers, W. T. & Bateson, D. J. (1991). The influence of test-wiseness on the performance of high school seniors on school leaving examinations. *Applied Measurement in Education, 4*, 159–183.

Roth, W. (1998). Situated cognition and assessment of competence in science. *Evaluation and Program Planning, 21*, 155–169.

Saloman, G. & Perkins, D. (1998). Individual and social aspects of learning. In *Review of Research in Education, 23*, 1–24.

Sarig, G. (1987). High-level reading in the first and in the foreign language: Some comparative process data. In J. Devine, P. L. Carrell, & D. E. Eskey (eds.), *Research in reading in English as a second language* (pp. 105–123). Washington, DC: TESOL.

Saville, N. (2000). Using observation checklists to validate speaking-test tasks. *Research Notes, 2* (August), pp. 16–17. Cambridge: University of Cambridge Local Examinations Syndicate.

Saville, N. & Kunnan, A. J. (2006). People and events in language testing: A sort of memoir: An interview with Bernard Spolsky. *Language Assessment Quarterly, 3*, 243–266.

Saville, N. & O'Sullivan, B. (2000). Developing observation checklists for speaking-tests. *Research Notes, 3* (November), pp. 6–10. Cambridge: University of Cambridge Local Examinations Syndicate.

Schegloff, E. A., Koshik, I., Jacoby, S. & Olsher, D. (2002). Conversation analysis and applied linguistics. *Annual Review of Applied Linguistics, 22*, 3–31.

Sfard, A. (1998). On two metaphors for learning and the dangers of choosing just one. *Educational Researcher, 27*(2), 4–13.

Shannon, C. E. & Weaver, W. (1963). *The mathematical theory of communication*. Urbana IL: University of Illinois Press.

Shohamy, E. (2001). *The power of tests: A critical perspective on the uses of language tests*. Harlow, UK: Pearson Educational.

Shohamy, E. (2006). *Language policy: Hidden agendas and new approaches*. London: Routledge.

Shohamy, E., Reves, T. & Bejerano, Y. (1986). Introducing a new comprehensive test of oral proficiency. *English Language Teaching Journal, 40*(3), 212–220.

Short, D. (1994). Expanding middle school horizons: Integrating language, culture and social studies. *TESOL Quarterly, 28*, 581–608.

Skehan, P. (1998). *A cognitive approach to language learning*. Oxford: Oxford University Press.

Snow, M. A. (2005). A model of academic literacy for integrated language and content instruction. In E. Hinkel (ed.), *Handbook of research in second language teaching and research*, pp. 693–712. Mahwah, NJ: Lawrence Erlbaum.

Solano-Flores, G. & Trumbull, E. (2003). Examining language in context: The need for new research and practice paradigms in the testing of English-language learners. *Educational Researcher, 32*(2), 3–13.

Song, W. (2004). Language learner strategy use and English proficiency on the Michigan English Language Assessment Battery (pp. 1–26). *Spaan Fellow Working Papers in Second or Foreign Language Assessment 3*. Retrieved October 20, 2006: www.lsa.umich.edu/UofM/Content/eli/document/ spaan_working_papers_v3_song.pdf.

Spolsky, B. (1967). Do they know enough English? In D. Wigglesworth (ed.), *ATESL Selected Conference Papers*. Washington, DC: NAFSA Studies and Papers, English Language Series.

Spolsky, B. (1971). Reduced redundancy as a language testing tool. In G. E. Perren & J. L. M. Trim (eds.), *Applications of linguistics: Selected papers of the Second International Congress of Applied Linguistics, Cambridge, September 1969* (pp. 383–390). Cambridge: Cambridge University Press.

Spolsky, B. (1973). What does it mean to know a language, or how do you get someone to perform his competence? In J. W. Oller Jr. & J. C. Richards (eds.), *Focus on the learner: Pragmatic perspectives for the language teacher* (pp. 164–176). Rowley, MA: Newbury House Publishers.

Spolsky, B. (1977). Language testing: Art or science. In G. Nickel (ed.), *Proceedings of the Fourth International Congress of Applied Linguistics* (pp. 7–28). Stuttgart: Hochschulverlag.

Spolsky, B. (1978). Introduction: Linguists and language testers. In B. Spolsky (ed.), *Approaches to language testing* (pp. v–x). Arlington, VA: Center for Applied Linguistics.

Spolsky, B. (1981). Some ethical questions about language testing. In C. Klein-Braley & D. Stevenson (eds.), *Practice and problems in language testing* (pp. 5–30). Frankfurt: Peter Lang.

Spolsky, B. (1984). The uses of language tests: An ethical envoi. In C. Rivera (ed.), *Placement procedures in bilingual education: Education and policy issues* (pp. 3–7). Clevedon, UK: Multilingual Matters Ltd.

Spolsky, B. (1985). What does it mean to know how to use a language: An essay on the theoretical basis of language testing. *Language Testing, 2*(2), 180–191.

Spolsky, B. (1995). *Measured words: The development of objective language testing.* Oxford: Oxford University Press.

Spolsky, B. (1996). Robert Lado, 1915–1995. *Language Testing Update, 19*, 66.

Spolsky, B. (1997). The ethics of gatekeeping tests: What have we learnt in a hundred years. *Language Testing, 14*(3), 242–247.

Spolsky, B. (2003). Review of *Continuity and Innovation. ELT Journal, 58*(3), 305–309.

Spolsky, B., Murphy, P., Holm, W. & Ferrel, A. (1971). Three functional tests of oral proficiency. *TESOL Quarterly, 6*, 221–235.

Spolsky, B., Sigurd, B., Sato, M., Walker, E. & Aterburn, C. (1968). Preliminary studies in the development of techniques for testing overall second language proficiency. *Language Learning, 3*, 79–101.

Stemmer, B. (1991). *What's on a C-test taker's mind? Mental processes in C-test taking.* Bochum: Universitätsverlag Dr. N. Brockmeyer.

Storey, P. (1997). Examining the test-taking process: A cognitive perspective on the discourse cloze test. *Language Testing, 14*(2), 214–231.

Swain, M. (1985). Large-scale communicative language testing: A case study. In Y. Lee, A. Fok, R. Lord & G. Low (eds.), *New directions in language testing* (pp. 35-46). Oxford: Pergamon.

Taguchi, N. (2001). L2 learners' strategic mental processes during a listening test. *JALT Journal, 23*(2), 176–201.

Tarone, E. (2000). Still wrestling with 'context' in interlanguage theory. *Annual Review of Applied Linguistics, 20*, 182–198.

Taylor, L. (2005). Using qualitative research methods in test development and validation. *Research Notes, 21* (August), pp. 2–4. Cambridge: University of Cambridge ESOL Examinations.

Taylor, W. S. (1953). Cloze procedures: A new tool for readability. *Journalism Quarterly, 30*, 415–433.

TechSmith. (2004). *Morae*. Okemos, MI: Techsmith Corporation. www.techsmith.com.

Test of English as a Foreign Language (TOEFL). (1964). Princeton, NJ: Educational Testing Service.

Test of English as a Foreign Language Internet Based Test (TOEFL iBT). (2005). Princeton, NJ: Educational Testing Service.

Test of Spoken English (TSE). (1979). Princeton, NJ: Educational Testing Service.

Test of Written English (TWE). (1986). Princeton, NJ: TOEFL/Educational Testing Service.

Thomas, W. & Collier, V. (1997). *School effectiveness for language minority education students*. Washington, DC: National Clearinghouse for Bilingual Education.

Thorndike, E. L. (1910). Handwriting. *Teachers College Record, 11*, 83–175.

Tian, S. (2000). *TOEFL reading comprehension: Strategies used by Taiwanese students with coaching-school training*. PhD dissertation, Teachers College, Columbia University.

Tomalin, C. (2003). *Samuel Pepys: The unequalled self*. London: Viking.

Tsagari, C. (1994). Method effect on testing reading comprehension: How far can we go? MA thesis, University of Lancaster. (ERIC Document Reproduction Service No. ED424768)

Upshur, J. (1979). Functional proficiency theory and a research role for language tests. In E. Brière & F. Hinofotis (eds.), *Concepts in language testing: Some recent studies* (pp. 75–100). Washington, DC: TESOL.

Upshur, J. & Turner, C. (1999). Systematic effects in the rating of second language speaking ability: Test method and learner discourse. *Language Testing, 16*, 82–111.

Valette, R. (1967). *Modern language testing: A handbook*. New York: Harcourt, Brace Jovanovich.

van Lier, L. (1989). Reeling, writhing, drawling, stretching, and fainting in coils: Oral proficiency interviews as conversation. *TESOL Quarterly, 23*, 489–508.

van Lier, L. (2004). *The ecology and semiotics of language learning: A sociocultural perspective*. Boston: Kluwer.

Vogely, A. J. (1998). Listening comprehension anxiety: Students' reported sources and solutions. *Foreign Language annals, 31*(1), 67–80.

Vollmer, H. (1980). A study of alternatives in explaining the general language proficiency factor. Paper presented at the Language Testing Research Colloquium, San Francisco.

Vollmer, H. & Sang, F. (1983). Competing hypotheses about second language ability: A plea for caution. In J. W. Oller, Jr. (ed.), *Issues in language testing research* (pp. 29–74). Rowley, MA: Newbury House.

Weir, C. (1981). Reaction to the Morrow paper (1). In J. C. Alderson & A. Hughes (eds.), *Issues in language testing* (pp. 26–37). London: British Council.

Weir, C. & Milanovic, M. (2003). *Continuity and innovation: Revising the Cambridge Proficiency in English Examination 1913–2002, Studies in Language Testing, 15*. Cambridge: UCLES/Cambridge University Press.

Wesche, M. (1987). Second language performance testing: The Ontario test of ESL as an example. *Language Testing, 4*(1), 28–47.

Wilds, C. (1975). The oral interview test. In B. Spolsky & R. L. Jones (eds.), *Testing language proficiency* (pp. 29–37). Washington, DC: Center for Applied Linguistics.

Wiley, E. & Ingram, D. E. (1995, 1999). *International Second Language Proficiency Ratings (ISLPR): General proficiency version for English.* Brisbane: Centre for Applied Linguistics and Languages, Griffith University.

Wu, Y. (1998). What do tests of listening comprehension test? A retrospection study of EFL test-takers performing a multiple-choice task. *Language Testing, 15*(1), 21–44.

Yang, P. (2000). *Effects of test-wiseness upon performance on the Test of English as a Foreign Language.* PhD dissertation, University of Alberta.

Yoshida-Morise, Y. (1998). The use of communication strategies in language proficiency interviews. In R. Young & A. W. He (eds.), *Talking and testing: Discourse approaches to the assessment of oral proficiency* (pp. 205–238). Amsterdam: John Benjamins.

Yoshizawa, K. (2002). *Relationships among strategy use, foreign language aptitude, and second language proficiency: A structural equation modeling approach.* PhD dissertation, Temple University.

Young, R. (2000). Interactional competence: Challenges for validity. Paper presented at the American Association for Applied Linguistics, Vancouver, BC.

Young, R. & He, A. W. (eds.). (1998). *Talking and testing: Discourse approaches to the assessment of oral proficiency.* Amsterdam: John Benjamins.

Zamel, V. & Spack, R. (eds.). (1998). *Negotiating academic literacies.* Mahwah, NJ: Erlbaum.

INDEX

Abanomey, A., 97
Abedi, J., 149
ability (*see* language ability)
achievement test, 105
Alderson, J. C., 2, 24, 26, 37, 38, 48, 51, 52
Alderson, J. C., N. Figueras, G. Nold,
 B. North, S. Takala, and C. Tardieu, 25, 26
Alderson, J. C. and A. Hughes, 44, 50
Allan, A., 102
American Council on the Teaching of Foreign
 Languages (ACTFL), 21–22, 57
Anderson, M. L, 65
Anderson, N. J, 96
Anderson, N. J, L. F. Bachman, K. Perkins,
 and A. Cohen, 96
Atkinson, J. M. and J. Heritage, 116, 127
authenticity, 29
  real-life, 43, 48, 51–52, 77–80, 86
    content/text, 96–97
    context, 48, 66
    tasks, 44, 45, 54, 56, 57

Bachman, L. F., 2, 3, 5, 16, 23, 31, 42, 43, 45,
 54–56, 58, 61–63, 66–68, 69, 70, 77, 95,
 113, 132, 133, 137
Bachman, L. F. and A. S. Palmer, 45, 54–56,
 58, 62
Bailey, A. and F. Butler, 74
Banerjee, J. and F. Franceschina, 37
Bennett, R., 38
Bialystok, E., 149
bias, 143 (*see also* fairness)
Brindley, G., 21, 22, 45, 56
Brindley, G. and H. Slatyer, 32
British Council, 10, 74, 77, 83
Broadfoot, P., 34, 35
Brown, A., 133
Brown, A. and T. McNamara, 133
Brown, J.D., T. Hudson, J. Norris, W. Bonk,
 45, 56
Butler, F. and R. Stevens, 35
Butler, J., 136
Byrnes, H., 137, 146

C-test, 10, 91, 94

Cambridge English Speakers of Other
 Languages (ESOL), 23, 83, 84, 115, 116,
 119, 121, 123,125, 126 (*see also* UCLES)
Campbell, D. T. and D. W. Fiske, 53
Canale, M., 44, 50
Canale, M. and M. Swain, 44, 49–50, 53–54,
 60, 143
Canagarajah, S., 151
Carroll, J. B., 11, 15, 44, 46–47, 77
Carroll, J. B., A. S. Carton, and C. Wilds, 10
Center for Applied Linguistics, 11
Certificate in Advanced English (CAE),
 116–119, 123–125
Chalhoub-Deville, M., 31, 32, 45, 61–65, 69
Chalhoub-Deville, M. and C. Deville, 61
Chalhoub-Deville, M. and E. Tarone, 70
Chamot, A. and J. O'Malley, 74
Chapelle, C., 45, 58, 59, 63, 65–66
Cheng, L., T. W. Rogers, and H. Hu, 33
Chomsky, N., 14, 46
Clapham, C., 77
Clark, J. L. D., 44, 48
classroom assessment, 2, 33–35, 62, 110,
 142–144
Clay, M., 33
cloze, 10, 48–49, 79, 91, 97–98, 105
Cohen, A. D., 4, 90–93, 106, 126
Cohen, A. D. and E. Aphek, 105
Cohen, A. D., and A. Brooks-Carson, 93–94
Cohen, A. D., and E. Macaro, 109
Cohen, A. D. and T. Upton, 98–99, 101
construct, 1, 3–4, 6, 21, 24–25, 28, 41–45,
 66–71, 78
  communicative language testing, 44, 49–55,
 73, 79–81
  direct/performance testing, 44, 47–48
  interactionalist, 31, 43, 45, 57–66, 68–69
  pragmatic, 44, 48–49
  structural (skills and elements), 44, 46–47,
 78–79, 81
  task-based performance assessment, 45,
 55–57
context
  ability-in-individual-in-context, 61–65
  co-construction, 31, 59–63

175

Printed and bound in May 2007
by TRI-GRAPHIC PRINTING LTD., Ottawa, Ontario,
for THE UNIVERSITY OF OTTAWA PRESS

Typeset in Adobe Times (Postscript) 10 on 12
by CARLETON PRODUCTION CENTRE, Ottawa, Ontario

Proofread by David Bernardi
Cover designed by Laura Brady

Printed on Enviro 100 White